W9-DES-213

THIS BOOK BELONGS TO:

PROOF

This publication is design to provide accurate and authoritative
information in regard to the subject matter covered. It is sold
with the understanding that the publisher is not engaged in
rendering legal, accounting or other professional service. If
legal advice or other expert assistance is required, the services
of a competent professional person should be sought.

Although the author has researched all sources to ensure the
accuracy and completeness of the information contained in
this book, we assume no responsibility for errors, inaccuracies,
omissions, or any inconsistency herein. Any slights of people
or organizations are unintentional. Readers are encouraged
to consult an attorney or CSEA caseworker for specific
applications to their individual situations.

The names in this book have been changed in each story to
protect the families involved but the stories are all real.

Email me your child support story to
                    dawnetteculp@yahoo.com

The Face of

CHILD SUPPORT

A step-by-step guide and workbook to establishing a
support order. For both custodial and noncustodial parents.

Dawnette Lounds-Culp

ISBN 0-9755346-0-2

5 1 6 9 5

9 780975 534601

**A N G E L E Y E S
PUBLISHING CO.,INC.**

DEDICATION

The Face of Child Support is dedicated to my husband, son, mother, sisters, and friends who have experienced and endured the negative effects of child support.

This book is to make certain that other custodial parents (men or women) are encouraged and educated to successfully obtain a support order and to ensure that a support order is enforced.

The Face of Child Support is also intended to inspire noncustodial parents to actively participate in the lives of their children and to commit to assisting their children financially by paying child support.

THANK YOU

The Face of Child Support would not have been possible if not for the support of my husband Steven, my son Austin and many of my family and friends that have personally experienced the child support process. When faced with this social issue myself, I had to rely on the support of a friend that had already gone through the process. If it were not for Allison who encouraged me to continue the process—no matter what, I would have not been able to provide the quality of life for my son. Also, I learned first hand from my mother and sisters how not receiving child support can affect my son.

After I successfully obtained a support order, I, too, became an inspiration to many friends and knew immediately that a guidebook would assist many more in the process. Special thanks to all my friends for allowing me to assist and motivate them to take action in their child support efforts.

Thanks to Pia Forbes for being instrumental in the editing of this book.

Thanks to The Office Of Child Support Enforcement and the state of Georgia Child Support Administration for allowing me to include their information in my book.

And a final thanks to you for purchasing The Face of Child Support.

TABLE OF CONTENTS

PREFACE

The Face of Child Support is a timeless guide that strengthens families when on parent is not at home. There are over 16 million caseloads totaling $20.1 billion collected in child support payments. The custodial parent and noncustodial parent are both vital in the development, physically and emotionally of their children. Historically, child support enforcement goal provided four major services to our customers: locating non-custodial parents, establishing paternity, establishing support orders and collecting support payments. Today, CSE continues to provide these services along with additional services to foster relationships between noncustodial parents and their children.

When on thinks about child support, the gender that is usually the custodial parent is the mother, however, more fathers are custodial parents. There were a total of 6,924,000 custodial parents in the 2001 Census Bureau, Current Population Survey, April 2002. Of this number, 712,000 were fathers that were custodial parents. The changing gender of child support still however increases the number of paternities that is established or acknowledged each year. The CSE program had 1.5 million paternities established or acknowledged, and 1.2 million new child support orders were established, according to the Office of Child Support Enforcement.

The goal of this book is to education, empower and encourage both custodial and noncustodial parents in actively participating in the lives of their children. Sometimes it seems unfair that CSE programs focuses more on the financial aspect of the wellbeing of children. The bottom line is that the financial state of a household provides a better way of life for our children. When one parent is not at home, the financial aspect of taking care of their children is absent. Therefore, the financial support is crucial. The Face of Child Support encourages the strengths of families, however, sometimes families are broken by divorces or were started out of wedlock, whatever the situation may be, the support of our children is the most important role we can play. Let's continue to work together in providing a better life for our children physically and emotionally.

A NOTE FROM THE AUTHOR

Are you a custodial parent or a non-custodial parent faced with the daily challenges of collecting child support, paying child support, keeping up with the changes in child support, raising or being involved with your child(ren) and trying to relate to the other parent all at the same time? I know how difficult it is juggling your daily life. That's the reason for <u>The Face of Child Support</u>: to empower, inform, educate, and navigate you successfully through your process and well after.

Knowledge is power. And when you learn that millions of other parents are going through or have already gone through the process, your desire to do what is right for your child will be strengthened.

Many people are faced with child support for one reason or the other. From billionaires to welfare recipients, no one is exempt. With this in mind, information in <u>The Face of Child Support</u> will provide the necessary know-how to keep you on top of the game in the child support process.

If you have not yet gone through the process, are dealing with or have already gone through the procedures, <u>The Face of Child Support</u> is for you. I encourage you to read through the pages and learn how both parents can be intimately involved in the child's life.

The Child Support Enforcement Agency (CSEA) has

taken a strong stance in supporting families. The Face of Child Support recognizes the powerful voice of the federal government, and I have included information from CSEA handbook to provide readers with the most up-to-date information pertaining to child support.

Because I am a recipient of child support and have gone through the process, I am acutely aware of what many custodial parents, noncustodial parents, and children are faced with day to day. The reason this book is important to me is because it provides a positive source for you to turn to, even when there is no one else to turn to.

Lastly, you will find the basic steps to follow to establish your child support case and obtain a support order, and to collect the support due, whether you are working with your state or local CSE program or your attorney.

This is for the millions of parents who put their children first by responsibly providing for their emotional and financial support...

Tell everyone that has a child and is contemplating, going through, or has gone through the child support process about The Face of Child Support. However, this book is instrumental in all phases of your process and is a must keep, so ask them to purchase their own copy of The Face of Child Support.

Thank you for your support,

INTRODUCTION

I knew firsthand about child support from childhood because my mother went through the ordeal with my father. They had a bitter divorce and in the end, my mother was awarded a small amount of child support for six children. All I remembered was that my mother always complained about my father not paying leaving us to live off her salary. The support order was for him to pay $15 per child, but it was easier to go out and work to support the family than to be aggravated or disappointed by him.

My mother received government assistance in the form of food stamps. We ate well, but there were many things that as children we would miss. I enjoyed going to the grocery store. I'd pick up the box of Twinkies and ask my mother, "can I have this?" She would always say yes. I watched my mother raise six children to the best of her abilities, and in hindsight, I wish the laws had worked to her advantage.

Though child support enforcement laws back then were limited, they have now changed for the better. As a single adult with a child, I did not have faith in the child support system. I knew that I would not be in the system or let a third party decide for me what I could work out with my son's father.

I knew the Child Support Enforcement (CSE) program was a federal/state/local partnership dedicated to collecting child support and sending the message that parents cannot walk away from their children. I also knew that CSE goals include fostering responsible behavior towards children and reducing welfare costs.

Still, my confidence in the system was limited, based on my mother's experience. I watched my mother work long hours and come home late at night, missing out on homework and school activities.

I resented my mother for not spending time with my sisters and me, not understanding that she had to work to make ends meet. In retrospect, I realize that my father was wrong for not paying child support. And now, many years later, I am faced with what my mother had to endure.

I made a great effort to keep up with my son's needs and wants. I wanted him to have the world, but what I could provide was limited. I realized then that it was just a repeat of my mother's life. I assumed the system would not assist me because they had not assisted her. I came to realize that child support enforcement provides hope as well as support to my son. I decided to put my son first by legally making his father responsibly provide for our son's emotional and financial needs.

I was always concerned that he would try to take Austin away from me to prevent paying child support. He had threatened me before and that always stayed in my mind. I had to learn my rights and responsibilities and stick to my plans.

I became wise about the process. Alex wanted Austin to live with him for a one-year period. I was very hesitant about this based on his prior threats to take Austin away from me. I was torn about the decision, but I never wanted to come between Austin and his father. His father had always played a role in his life. I never had a problem with the time Alex spent with Austin or ever doubted his love for his son. To make myself comfortable, I drafted a written agreement between the two of us, outlining the specifics. I wrote a letter to Alex, specifying me as the custodial parent and him as the caretaker for a period of one year. He signed it and the document became legal.

The child support process is very intense, involved, and time consuming, but the steps are predictable. My story is interesting; however, to provide a full scope of what others may go through, I have invited some of my friends to assist me in telling their stories. In each chapter, you will find information from the Child Support Enforcement Agency Handbook to provide you with precise detail on the topic discussed.

What is important to know is that everyone facing child support will experience, in part, something similar. I remember being so full of hurt, feeling betrayed and alone, feeling like giving up. Allison, a good friend, gave me perspective by simply saying that she had gone through the same thing. Her reaction was different than mine, but we both went through the same ordeal, and sharing it with her made it much easier.

ABOUT CHILD SUPPORT

In spite of stronger laws, millions of children are still deprived of the support they need and deserve. The collection of child support is crucial to helping families attain self-sufficiency.

The CSE program was established in 1975 as Title IV-D of the Social Security Act. It functions in all states and territories through the state/county Social Services Department, Attorney General's Office, or Department of Revenue. Most states work with prosecuting attorneys, other law enforcement agencies, and officials of family or domestic relations courts to carry out the program at the local level.

The Federal Office of Child Support Enforcement is part of the U.S. Department of Health and Human Services. It helps states develop, manage, and operate their programs effectively and according to Federal law. The office pays the major share of state program operating costs, provides policy guidance and technical help to enforcement agencies, conducts audits and educational programs, supports research, and shares ideas for program improvement.

Child support enforcement services are required for families receiving assistance under the Temporary Assistance for Needy Families (TANF) program. In addition, child support services are available to families not receiving TANF who apply for such services, as well as families who were formerly on TANF. Current child support payments collected on behalf of former TANF families are distributed to the families. Child support payments collected on behalf of non-TANF families are also forwarded to the families.

For the most part, child support enforcement problems are handled according to state and local laws and practices. States often can use administrative procedures or other legal processes for establishing and enforcing support orders more quickly than is usually possible with court proceedings.

Your state's Child Support Enforcement program is available to help you 1) find the noncustodial parent (Location); 2) establish legal fatherhood for children (Paternity); 3) establish the legal support order (Obligation); and 4) collect child support payments (Enforcement).

Problems such as property settlement, visitation, and custody are not, by themselves, child support enforcement issues and the CSE program generally cannot enforce court orders relating to them. Parents must deal with these issues through the courts or other systems set up by the state. Today, about 85 percent of custodial parents are women and 15 percent of custodial parents are men. Either parent may be awarded primary custody by the court.

Provisions in the 1996 bipartisan welfare reform legislation strengthened and improved state child support collection activities by establishing a national new hire and wage reporting system, streamlining paternity establishment, creating uniform interstate child support forms, computerizing statewide collections, and authorizing tough new penalties for nonpayment, such as driver's license revocation.

NOTES

THE EMOTIONS OF BOTH PARENTS

Before I get into the nitty gritty of the book, I want to speak about the psychological dilemma a custodial and noncustodial parent may go through.

Fathers, in the past, could only hope for custody by convincing the court that the mother was unfit to care for the children. Courts now consider what's in the best interest of the children when deciding upon the custodial parent. In deciding custody, more and more courts are looking to determine which parent is the more active caregiver-that is, the one whom the child relies upon most for day-to-day care.

As a custodial mother going through the child support process, the emotional and psychological affects are varied. My feelings were initially of guilt, fear, betrayal, frustration and hurt. Once in the system and needing to attain the knowledge to maneuver through the system, I then felt in control. There were times when the process was taking too long and I felt discouraged. I must admit that the most exhilarating feeling was that of being empowered to take control of my son's life.

As a noncustodial parent, some of the emotional and psychological feelings are universal: hurt, betrayal, anger and frustration. Sometimes, the ones paying child support feel like an outside force has more say so in the life of their child than they do. Some feel like a criminal because they are always being scrutinized and watched based on how much money they make. And some are so fed up that they feel as the system was designed for the custodial parent and out to get them.

I have a friend who is a great guy. He is a noncustodial father with little or no contact with his teenage son who lives in another state. He was once married but was forced into marriage because she had gotten pregnant and had threatened him with abortion. After several years of marriage and feeling trapped and being manipulated, he left the marriage and his son. The great thing about my friend is that he faithfully gave his ex-wife money each month to support his son. When faced with going through the divorce, his attorney said the only issue that would prevent the divorce from happening expediently was the issue of child support. Wanting nothing from the marriage but wanting to do the right thing and support his son, he went to the child support office and put himself on child support. Once there and in the system, he felt less than a human; he felt as though he had just placed himself in prison. The payment wound up being less than what he was paying her on his own, yet he felt like he was a criminal.

The documents he received and had to complete were negative: "you are ordered to...", the punishment when you...," " if you don't start immediately, if you miss a payment, the recourse is..." He became bitter and resented the child support enforcement system. To make matters worse, his ex-wife would not let himvisit his son. She would make excuses when he would come in town. She would say bad things about him around his son and his son began to resent him, too. He felt so hopeless as he told me his story. I felt compelled to write about him because not all noncustodial parents are trying not to pay and more are trying to be involved in the lives of their children.

Matthew felt that the system was out to get him. He said that he never understood why people came up with these notions until he experienced it himself. I explained to him that the system was designed to accommodate neither the custodial nor the noncustodial parent. The system was designed to decrease the number of families receiving support from the government.

MY EMOTIONS ARE:

NOTES

DECIDING TO FILE FOR CHILD SUPPORT

It's not an easy decision to take the other parent of your child to court to make him pay for his responsibility. It took me until my son was six to finally go through the court process. It didn't start like that though. I had had an intelligent conversation with my son's father about his financial responsibilities and we came to an agreement, I was so proud of myself. I did not have to go through that lengthy process and most importantly, I did not have a third party involved.

Per our agreement for him to pay every other week, we planned a spring break trip to go to Disney World with one of my son's friend. We strategically planned the trip the week that child support was due. The week came, we packed our bags, my girlfriend came to my house to pick us up to begin our road trip to Disney World. The child support had not come. I called my son's father to see where the money was and he said that the check was in the mail. I told him that the check should have been there and that we had planned a trip based on receiving child support.

We did go to Disney World without the child support.

The check did not come until several days after we had gotten back from our trip. He had lied. This happened for several months. I had to make long distance phone calls every two weeks to find out what happened to the child support payment. The same excuse: the check is in the mail.

I finally decided to stop being a bill collector. I stopped calling, and the checks stop coming. About one year later, I decided that my decision not to establish a support order through the state was very unfair to my son. I realized that I was taking away from my son by him not having the financial support of his father. Finally, I realized that the financial support of my son was of the utmost importance to me. Having a child is a shared responsibility, and if my son's father was shirking his responsibility, I would have to put him in the system.

I hadn't a clue what I needed to do. As fate would have it, I sublet an office in a building that had a private agency that established child support for custodial parents. I visited the office to find out what I needed to do to pursue child support for my son. They gave me a list of things, and I set out to gather the information. This was a private agency supported by the state's Child Support Enforcement program. Even though each state provides public and private services, one can elect to use an attorney to establish an order. Let me explain the difference:

PUBLIC AGENCY

The state government operates a public child support enforcement agency. There are many agencies throughout the states operating in different counties and rural areas. The Child Support Enforcement (CSE) program is run by the state's Human Services Department, Attorney General's Office, or Department of Revenue. Public agencies have caseworkers that assist each case in obtaining a support order. Using a public agency may take longer.

PRIVATE AGENCY

A private agency can establish child support orders and is under the auspices of the state's CSE programs. There may be a fee associated in using a private agency. Private agencies also have caseworkers that assist each case in obtaining a support order.

ATTORNEY

There are many law offices and private attorneys that specialize in child support cases. Using your own attorney can result in reaching an order quicker than using a public or private agency. However, these attorneys and law offices charge a fee for their services. These fees can amount to thousands of dollars based on the length of time spent on each case\ as well as how much information they need to gather to present each case.

CHILD SUPPORT VS. VISITATION

One of my concerns with deciding to file for child support was Alex's threat of taking Austin away from me. I knew that he would have visitation rights and when he was with him, he would keep him. I was not aware, as most parents are not aware, that establishing a child support order has nothing to do with visitation rights. I had a friend who was a judge and he gave me information. From the information I gathered and perused, it gave me the encouragement to move forward.

Although the CSE program lacks authority to enforce visitation, many state or local governments have developed procedures for enforcing visitation orders. Also, a provision of the Personal Responsibility and Work Opportunity Reconciliation Act of 1996 (PRWORA) makes funding available to states for developing model programs to ensure that children will be able to have the continuing care and emotional support of both parents. This was my concern and I found out that my CSE office had resources available to me and had laws that address custody and visitation. My extensive research and the information that I had gathered assisted a friend in her decision. It's amazing how when I attain information about child support enforcement, immediately someone else needs the same information.

ANN'S STORY
Ann came to me to discuss her children's father not paying child support. She had no idea that I had done intensive research on the subject. She told me that her two sons' father lived in another state and had not paid child support since they separated. She had moved to Atlanta to start her life over with her two sons. She kept in contact with the father, and the children spent two weeks each summer with him. But, she was struggling to make

ends meet and she needed assistance in daycare and extra curricular activities for her two athletic boys. She went on and on and on, and I knew too well this story. It was like I had tape recorded myself and pushed play.

She was sincere and needed assistance. I began to ask her personal questions, and she had all the pertinent information. I then asked her if she wanted to file for a support order. She said the decision was not an easy one but a necessary one. She was certain and was ready to take the next step. I told her to contact the county in which they lived before to start the process. Two weeks later, she excitedly reported starting the process. She was so thankful and so amazed by how easy it was.

MY REASONS FOR FILING.

NOTES

FILING FOR CHILD SUPPORT

I did it! I filed for child support. I gathered all my information and went to a private CSE office. I waited patiently for my name to be called. A woman introduced herself to me when I signaled that it was my name she called. We went into a private room where we sat and talked. I shared with her my story. I opened my folder and also shared my information with her. She commended me for doing my homework and confirmed that the information I provided to her would allow her to obtain a support order quicker. Since it was an out-of-state case, it would take a little longer. I had waited six years; I had nothing to loose by waiting any longer.

There was a packet of information that I had to complete. The forms asked information such as whether I had received government assistance in the past, the identity of the father, his address and social security number, my address and social security number, where our child was born, whether the father's name was on the birth certificate, and the last time of contact with the father. I completed the questions and was relieved when the interview was over. I had successfully started the child support process and had a file with the CSE office. I left that office feeling so empowered, so in control.

I went home and celebrated by preparing my son's favorite meal. I did not inform my son or his father as to my actions that day. I just waited for the course to unfold.

I must say, it took much longer than I expected. It

wasn't all because of the interstate case; it was because Alex thought he was smart. He hired a private attorney to represent him in his child support case. I was very disappointed because he was spending unnecessary money by retaining an attorney to represent him in a simple case. The steps of child support are standard and concise, and determining the payment amount uses a standardized system. I grew more bitter with each day. On the worst days, though, when I thought of child support, it was my son's face that I saw.

I got bitter, but I got smarter. I had time on my side. I became patient. I became totally involved in the case. I knew that in the end, our son would be living a better life. I was not giving up. It was full speed ahead. It was time to sit back and relax, sit back and watch what was inevitable. I became wise and depended on the system that I once doubted.

I mentioned earlier that the Child Support Enforcement program provides four major services to its customers: locating non-custodial parents, establishing paternity, establishing support orders and collecting support payments. The program also provides services to non-custodial parents. States offer access and visitation services through Federal grants.

Locating Non-Custodial Parents – Child support enforcement officials can use information from highly computerized state and Federal Parent Locator Services (FPLS) to locate parents.

Establishing Paternity – Legally identifying a child's father is called paternity establishment. This is the necessary first step for obtaining an order for child support when a child is born out of wedlock. Establishing paternity can also provide a child with access to Social Security benefits, pension and retirement benefits; medical insurance and health information; and important interactions and relationships with both parents.

Establishing Support Orders – States must have guidelines to determine how much a parent should pay for child support. Child support orders can be established by a court or by an administrative hearing process. Provisions for health insurance coverage must be included in the support order.

Collecting Support – A parent can be required to pay child support by income withholding. Over 60 percent of all child support is paid by income withholding. Overdue child support can be collected from federal and state income tax refunds. Liens can be placed on property, and the property itself can be sold to pay back child support owed. Unpaid child support can be reported automatically to credit reporting bureaus. Drivers, professional, occupational and recreational licenses can be suspended if the obligated parent is not paying required support. The U.S. State Department will deny a passport to someone who owes more than $5000 in back child support. Child support agencies have agreements with financial institutions to freeze and seize accounts of those identified as owing back child support.

States have uniform interstate laws to make it easier to collect support across state lines. There are registries of newly hired employees to speed collection of support. There is also a special effort, in certain states and under certain circumstances, where criminal actions can be taken against chronic delinquent parents who owe large sums of child support.

Services for Non-Custodial Parents — States receive grants from the federal government to help with non-custodial parents access to and visitation with their children. Each state operates such programs under very broad guidelines. These projects can provide mediation, counseling, parenting education, visitation programs, and the development of visitation and custody guidelines. There are also projects in a number of states to promote responsible fatherhood and encourage marriage.

To apply for child support services, call your local CSE office. Check the county listings in your telephone book to get the telephone number. To be eligible for assistance, you must provide information to help to identify the father and collect child support from him. Any child support collected will be used to help support your children—going either directly to you or to repay the state for your assistance grant. Your state CSE agency will explain how the child support will be used.

State CSE offices charge an application fee of not more than $25 for non-AFDC (Aid to Families with Dependent Children) cases, although some states absorb all or part of the fee. AFDC recipients do not have to pay for child support enforcement services. The Department of Justice does not charge a fee for prosecuting criminal nonsupport cases.

PIPER'S STORY

When I was writing this book, I had an interesting conversation with a friend, Piper. I was informing her about my project and what I was so intently involved in. I told her about The Face of Child Support project. She looked so shocked and so relieved at the same time that I could only guess that she was going through the child support decision. She had just decided to file for child support after having put her husband out over three years before.

She asked me the same question I asked myself: Why do custodial parents wait until we are absolutely in an awkward situation to file? Like me and like Piper, most get tired of waiting for them to do the right thing. We discussed how other custodial parents may feel and this is what we brainstormed:

Custodial Parents:
• may feel that the noncustodial parent will come back into their lives

- may feel threatened by the noncustodial parent.
- think that the noncustodial parent will eventually pay
- just accept the little amount that they receive from the noncustodial parent
- don't know where the other parent is
- are exhausted from the lengthy process of filing for support
- feel that most government institutions treat them like second class citizens
- are disgusted about the long wait for the process to finally come to fruition
- want to show the other parent they can do it alone

In Piper's case, she was mad, angry, hurt, and disappointed that her husband had betrayed her.

Piper was married for sixteen years and had two girls, ages sixteen and fourteen. Piper had suspected that her husband had been unfaithful. One Father's Day weekend, he did the unthinkable; he stayed away the entire weekend with not even a phone call to his family. Fed up with his actions, she put him out.

For two years after Piper put her husband out, he had no contact with her or his two girls. Piper knew that he lived about ten miles away. The girls had a father/daughter dance and they wanted him to be there with them. The girls felt abandoned, so they wrote a letter requesting his presence at the father/daughter dance. He attended the dance and has been actively in contact with his children. However, the financial responsibility of caring for two teenage girls had caught up with Piper. She told me that she had downloaded the application to file for child support but had not completed the form. I volunteered to help her, and together we completed them. She submitted the paperwork to the local CSE office.

STEPS I MUST TAKE TO FILE.

NOTES

WHO CAN APPLY FOR CHILD SUPPORT ENFORCEMENT?

Any parent or person with custody of a child who needs help to establish a child support or medical support order or to collect support payments can apply for child support enforcement services. People who have received assistance under cash assistance programs - Aid to Families with Dependent Children (AFDC), the new Temporary Assistance for Needy Families (TANF), Medicaid, or Federally-assisted Foster Care program-are automatically referred for child support enforcement services.

An unmarried father can apply for services to establish paternity-a legal relationship with his child.

A noncustodial parent whose case is not in the CSE program can request services to make payments through the program. Doing so can ensure that there is a record of payments made.

THE COSTS INVOLVED IN THE CHILD SUPPORT PROCESS

Because child support agencies may recover all or part of the actual costs of their services from customers who are not in a public assistance program, there may be other costs to parents. These can include the cost of legal work done by agency attorneys and costs for locating a noncustodial parent. Such costs may be deducted from the child support before it is sent to you or may be collected from the noncustodial parent. Not all states recover the costs of their services.

Your local CSE office can tell you about the practices in your state or visit our website, angeleyespublishingco. com to link to your state's CSE office.

Your caseworker should be able to estimate the costs involved in your case and give you an idea of how much they will deduct from each check before sending it to you. If you have not received cash assistance, you will receive the total child support payment (less any fees the state may collect). If you are receiving cash assistance, check with your state's CSE agency. Some states will give you the entire child support payment and reduce your assistance payment; others will keep the entire amount and not reduce the assistance payment. If you are not receiving cash assistance now but did in the past, if amounts are still owed to the state, any support collected beyond the amount ordered for current support may be used to reduce the arrearages owed.

There may be extra costs if more than one state is handling your case. Ask your caseworker to estimate these costs, if any.

CSE offices are required to monitor payments to make sure they are made regularly and fully. But you should inform the agency if payments are late or in the wrong amount, or if you receive payments directly. When monitor your case, you can keep the CSE office informed so that it can act quickly if needed.

If you are the noncustodial parent paying child support, you should send your payment to whoever is specified in the child support order. Since January 1994, support orders must include a provision for wage withholding unless both parents and the courts agree on another payment method. If your order does not call for wage withholding, you can request this service. If you do, you will have a record that you have made payments as required. If you are self-employed, you may be able to arrange for an automatic transfer of funds to the child support agency by way of electronic funds transfer. Either parent can apply for CSE services, which include receiving and distributing payments.

Don't be discouraged if the noncustodial parent lives out of town. Most local CSE offices handle enforcement in different jurisdictions in the same state without your having to travel outside your own jurisdiction. This eliminates any cost you could have incurred for traveling to and from the location of the noncustodial parent. Ask your local CSE office for details about how enforcement would work in your case.

Filing for child support is to provide a better life for our children, a better life in which their development, safety, and mental stimulation is encouraged. Some parents are faced with hostile and brutal noncustodial parents where children should be protected. Under these and other conditions of concern, the CSE office may agree that there is "good cause" for not trying to collect support from the father. You can explain the situation to your caseworker and provide supporting information.

Many mothers cannot sustain a household without the financial support of the noncustodial parent. Be encouraged that while waiting for child support payments to be received, you can get cash assistance if you are trying to help find the noncustodial parent. Your state or local CSE agency will tell you what information they will need you to provide in order to get assistance.

No matter where you start--establishing paternity, finding a noncustodial parent, or establishing or enforcing a support order--the CSE office must have enough information to pursue your case. All information you provide will be treated in confidence. The more details you provide, the easier it will be to process your case and to collect child support payments for your children.

NOTES

INTERSTATE AND INTERNATIONAL COOPERATION

When I met Alex, we both lived in Atlanta. Our child was born in Atlanta. However, Alex moved to another town to continue his education. Still, he was actively involved in his son's life, making time for Austin around his study time.

Then I got the phone call telling me that he was moving back to his hometown that was out of state. I did not know the value of having a father close in proximity to his son, but time would reveal how important it was.

When I decided to file for child support, I had to take in account that Alex lived in a different state. I did not know the child support laws there. Each state has its own laws, so I had to do more homework to compare both states and to gather the information that would make the process quicker and smoother. I was not going to allow the geographical difference between us deter me from filing. I found the information that I needed and pursued the interstate case. I was not prepared mentally for the emotional rollercoaster and the time it took, but I had to believe in the system and work extra hours to make up the difference.

When a caseworker was assigned to the case in the state in which Alex lived, I contacted that person and worked with them. I learned who the prosecuting attorney was, and I contacted her. We developed a close relationship and most of the time, she would contact me first about any changes on the case. I supplied her with all the information she would need. I then would contact my caseworker in my state to update them. I had to become actively involved in my case because the caseworkers would change just about every three months. I felt that my case would get lost in the piles of files they had. I knew that Alex was smart, and I had to keep one step ahead of the case.

The most difficult child support cases to pursue are those in which the parent obligated to pay child support lives in one state and the child and custodial parent live in another. However, all states are required to pursue child support enforcement, including location, paternity establishment, and establishment of support obligations, as vigorously for children who live outside their borders as for those under their own jurisdiction.

State enforcement agencies must cooperate with each other in handling requests for assistance; however, it has not been a simple matter for one state to automatically enforce the court orders of another state. Until recently, states used all or parts of a law called the Uniform Reciprocal Enforcement of Support Act (URESA).

With the enactment of the Full Faith and Credit For Child Support Orders Act and the federal mandate that all states enact the Uniform Interstate Family Support Act (UIFSA) by January 1, 1998, interstate enforcement of child support obligations should improve. UIFSA includes a provision designed to ensure that, when more than one state is involved, there is only one valid child support order which can be enforced for current support, as well as a provision which allows a state to work a case against an out-of-state obligor directly if certain conditions are met.

Both URESA and UIFSA have procedures under which an enforcement official (or private attorney) can refer a case for action in another state. The laws can be used to establish paternity and to establish, modify, or enforce a support order. A URESA state is able to refer a case to a UIFSA state and vice versa.

Interstate wage withholding can be used to enforce a support order in another state if the noncustodial parent's employer is known. With interstate wage withholding, the CSE office in the state where the noncustodial parent lives will make sure that a wage withholding order from another state contains all the information required by their state laws and will forward it to the noncustodial parent's employer. The order does not have to go through the courts as it would with an interstate child support enforcement petition. State laws vary and you will need to ask your caseworker whether this option is available in your case.

All state CSE agencies have an office called the Central Registry to receive incoming interstate child support cases, make sure that the information given is complete, send them to the right local office, and respond to inquiries from out-of-state CSE offices. Standard forms make it easier for caseworkers to find the information they need to enforce a case and to be sure they are supplying enough information for another state to enforce their case.

With interstate cases, even when you have adequate information regarding the noncustodial parent, any number of things can delay obtaining a support order: enforcement officials may not be able to serve notice on the noncustodial parent due to inadequate address information, or if a hearing is necessary, it may take a while to get a court date. In any of these instances, continue to keep in touch with your caseworker to resolve any delay or to provide any new information you may have.

The fact that you and the alleged father live in different states will not keep you from pursuing a paternity establishment action. Your state may be able to claim jurisdiction and establish paternity if the alleged father ever lived there or the child was conceived in your state. Otherwise, your state can petition the other state to establish paternity under their laws. Often, genetic tests will be ordered to help prove paternity. Ask your caseworker for specific information about the laws in your state and the state where the other parent lives.

A responding state's CSE office should not dismiss a case without asking for the information it needs. The initiating state is required to provide that information in 30 days. Either party in a contested paternity action can request blood or genetic testing. Ask your caseworker to reopen the case. You have the right to establish paternity until your child's 18th birthday.

Enforcement agencies have a very high demand for

their services. You may have to wait several months for the enforcement agency to get a reply to itsrequest for location assistance in another state. A state's ability to act rapidly depends on the characteristics of the case, the quality of information received, and the amount of staff and other resources they have to devote to it. Be sure to follow up regularly with your caseworker to make sure that each state is actively working your case.

Many custodial parents are angry when, after the noncustodial parent is finally located and served notice of the enforcement action, he or she moves. It is difficult to enforce child support payments when the noncustodial parent intentionally moves to avoid paying. Try to be an active participant in your own case. Whenever you learn that the noncustodial parent has moved or has a new job, you should tell your caseworker as soon as possible. As of October 1997, all states are required to have a State Directory of New Hires, and employers will be required to report hiring new employees within 20 days. The information will, in turn, be sent to a National Directory of New Hires. This helps in locating the noncustodial parent if he/she moves on to a new job.

The Child Support Recovery Act of 1992 makes it a federal crime to willfully fail to pay support for a child living in another state. In order to prosecute under this Act, the United States Attorney's Office must prove that the noncustodial parent was financially able to meet his/her obligation at the time the payment was due. If support arrearages are more than $5,000 or are unpaid for longer than one year, the noncustodial parent is subject to punishment. A major consideration in screening a case for federal prosecution is whether all reasonably available civil and state criminal remedies have been pursued first. Next, priority is given to cases: (1) where there is a pattern of moving from state to state to avoid payment; (2) where there is a pattern of deception (e.g., use of false name or social security number); (3) where there is failure to make support payments after being held in contempt of court; and (4) where failure to make support payments is connected to some other Federal offense such as bankruptcy fraud.

An interstate CSE action may be filed on your behalf to enforce your child support order. Before requesting that the other state attach this property, your enforcement worker or lawyer should see if a "withhold and deliver" or "attachment" of the property could be successfully carried out from your state.

Location and enforcement services may cost more if the CSE agency is dealing with another state. It depends on what the CSE office has to do to find the noncustodial parent and to establish regular payment. The more solid information and leads you provide, the more efficiently your case can be conducted. For non-assistance cases, states vary in the fees they charge for services. Your caseworker should be able to tell you more about these costs in your particular case.

If you don't have a support order, you can have one established by petitioning the court where the noncustodial parent lives. Your CSE office can also do this. Depending on the facts, it could be handled in your state or referred to another state under URESA or UIFSA. An affidavit of the facts, including the name and address of the responsible parent, details of your financial circumstances, and the needs of the child will be included. The petition will be mailed to the enforcement agency, the court, or the interstate official where the father lives. The responding state will review this information, together with information about the father's ability to pay, and set the amount to be paid.

You can still get a court order for child support enforced if the noncustodial parent has left the United States. I suggest you check with your local CSE office and state CSE agency (at the address listed in the back of this book). Many states' CSE agencies have agreements with foreign countries to recognize child support judgments made in other countries or to help establish orders when there is none. The U.S. Government is in the process of negotiating federal-level reciprocity declarations with other countries on behalf of all U.S. jurisdictions. These international child support agreements specify procedures for establishing and enforcing child support orders across borders. While requirements for getting enforcement action may vary depending on the other nation involved, a parent will be asked to provide the same information as in a domestic case, including as much specific information, such as address and employer of the noncustodial parent, as possible.

When the noncustodial parent works for an American company or for a foreign company with offices in the United States, wage withholding might work even if the country he lives in does not have any agreement to enforce an American state's order. Even in cases where the noncustodial parent is living and working in a country that has no reciprocity agreement, approaching the foreign employer directly for help might prove successful.

If the noncustodial parent lives in a country that has no agreement with any state to enforce child support obligations, the Office of Citizens Consular Services may be able to give you information about how to have the support order enforced in that country and how to obtain a list of attorneys there. That address is: Department of State, Office of Citizens Consular Services, Washington, D.C. 20520.

If a noncustodial parent is planning to live abroad and owes back child support, there is something the CSE office can do. Under the Personal Responsibility and Work Opportunity Reconciliation Act of 1996 (PRWORA) legislation, state CSE agencies can certify child support arrearages of more than $5000 to the Secretary of Health and Human Services, who, in turn, will transmit the certification to the Secretary of State for denial, revocation, or limitation of passports. This became effective October 1, 1997.

NOTES

INSIDE THE CSE AGENCY

When I visited the child support office in Atlanta, the number of people trying to establish a support order or following up on a support order overwhelmed me. My first instinct was to leave. Being there embarrassed me, but I completed the application package and returned it to the receptionist behind a glass window. The office took up the entire top floor of the 30-story office building. The caseworker approached me from a secured door and we met in a cubicle in a private room in the waiting area. I had not seen the work area of the caseworker, and I didn't know how many caseworkers were employed with the company. However, I knew that these caseworkers had more than their share of work.

I later learned that the typical CSEA office consists of about 50 caseworkers with an average caseload of 2500 each.

The work involved in each case is very demanding and challenging. The average number of cases per state may have is 450,000, with eight states that have over one million cases. The caseworkers are constantly changing, being replaced by new caseworkers looking to take on the challenges. The changing of caseworkers in my case always amazed me. I would call to give updates on my case, and I frequently got a new person working on my case. I'd develop a relationship with each caseworker to let them know how involved I was in my case. They respected my candid approach and welcomed any information I provided to them. This assisted in making their job easier.

Imagine all that is involved in their daily work. First, they have to compile all this information on at least three individuals; the mother, the father and the child involved in each case. Sometimes there are multiple children involved. To complicate matters, some mothers do not know who the fathers are, and the caseworkers have to track down more than one potential father to establish paternity. That's just the beginning. Once paternity is established, the caseworker has to locate the noncustodial parent. Then the casework has to take this person to court and endure the legal aspect of child support. Then when a support order is established, caseworkers have to enforce the order. It is an ongoing process.

A note from the Author:

I had a friend to read this section and she said it was discouraging. The information in this section was not mentioned to discourage you. Instead, it is the truth and to obtain a support order, you will have to understand the process and have patience. Stick with it; you will successfully make it through!

NOTES

THE PHASES OF COLLECTING
CHILD SUPPORT

The first phase of collecting child support is to locate the noncustodial parent. If you apply for services, the CSE office will try to find the noncustodial parent to establish or enforce a child support obligation. Be sure to give your caseworker all the information you have that might help find the parent.

The second phase, if a child was born out of wedlock, is to establish paternity - or make a legal determination of who fathered the child. Many men will voluntarily acknowledge paternity. Either parent can request a blood test in contested paternity cases. Your caseworker or attorney will help you to establish paternity for your child.

Establishing the obligation is the next phase. The fair amount of child support that the noncustodial parent should pay is determined according to state guidelines. Your CSE office will be able to tell you how support award amounts are set in your state. Your CSE office can also request medical support for your child.

The last phase is enforcement of the child support order. The CSE office can help with collecting the money due no matter where the noncustodial parent lives.

At any of these phases, the CSE office may need to know where the non-custodial parent is living or where he/she is working. When a parent has disappeared, it is usually possible for the CSE office to find him/her with the help of state agencies, such as the Department of Motor

Vehicles, or the Federal Parent Locator Service. Your caseworker can tell you what information is needed to find an absent parent or his/her employer.

The more you know about child support enforcement and the more you take an active role in getting information to your caseworker and asking questions about your case, the more success you will have in obtaining regular and full child support payments for your children.

WHICH PHASE ARE YOU IN?

PHASE ONE

LOCATION:
FIND THE NONCUSTODIAL PARENT

When I decided to file for child support, I needed Alex's address to expedite the process. I did not know, so I asked. He gave it to me and I filed it with the office of CSE.

When children are involved, custodial parents should make all effort to obtain as much information about the noncustodial parent when one leaves. It is not easy to track someone down without knowing pertinent information about them such as SSN, place of employment, or an address.

Most parents are unaware of where the noncustodial parent lives or works. It is important to know that locating the noncustodial parent is a crucial part of establishing a support order in a child support case. When one person makes a legal claim against another, the defendant must be given notice of the legal action taken and the steps necessary to protect his or her rights. To notify the noncustodial parent in advance—either by certified mail or in person—child support enforcement officials need a correct address. If you do not have the address, the CSE office can try to find it. The most important information that you can provide to the child support office is the noncustodial parent's social security number (SSN), making it less difficult to track them down.

The following information and documents will help the CSE office to locate the parent, establish paternity, and establish and/or enforce your child support order:

- Name, address and social security number
- Name and address of current or recent employer
- Names of friends and relatives
- Names of organizations to which he or she might belong
- Information about his or her income and assets – pay stubs, tax returns, bank statements, investments or property holdings
- Physical description
- Children's birth certificates
- Written statements (letters or notes) in which the alleged father has said or implied that the child is his (if paternity is an issue)
- Your child support order
- Your divorce decree or separation agreement
- Records of any child support received in the past
- Information about your income and assets

State CSE agencies, with due process and security safeguards, have access to information from the following:

- State and local government:
- Vital statistics
- State tax files
- Real and titled personal property records
- Occupational and professional licenses and business information
- Employment security agency
- Public assistance agency
- Motor vehicle department
- Law enforcement departments

- Records of private entities like public utilities and cable television companies (such as names and addresses of individuals and their employers as they appear in customer records)
- Information held by financial institutions, including asset and liability data

If you don't have the SSN, there are other ways to obtain it. Social Security Numbers are now required on applications for professional licenses, commercial driver's licenses, and marriage licenses, divorce records, support orders, paternity determinations or acknowledgements, and death records.

If none of these are available, or the SSN was not required when the document was issued, the CSE office can subpoena information about bank accounts, insurance policies, credit cards, pay stubs, or income tax returns. If you and the other parent filed a joint Federal income tax return in the last three years, the CSE office can get the social security number from the IRS. Your caseworker may be able to get the SSN with at least three of the following pieces of information: the parent's name, place of birth, date of birth, his/her father' name, and his/her mother's maiden name.

If the noncustodial parent cannot be found locally, your CSE office will ask the State Parent Locator Service (SPLS) to search. Using the SSN, the SPLS will check the records of state agencies such as motor vehicle registration, unemployment insurance, income tax, and correctional facilities. If the SPLS finds that the parent has moved to another state, it can ask the other state to search, or send a request to the Federal Parent Locator Service (FPLS).

The FPLS can search for addresses in the records of the Internal Revenue Service, the Department of Defense, the National Personnel Records Center, the Social Security Administration, the Department of Veterans Affairs, and State Employment Security Agencies. States will be reporting newly hired employees to a National Directory of New Hires, which, as of October 1, 1997, will be a part of the FPLS.

When working with a lawyer, you or your lawyer cannot ask the FPLS to find an address for the other parent. However, you or your attorney can submit a request to use the FPLS through the local or state CSE agency.

The state and federal location efforts can be made at the same time. For instance, a search can be initiated, simultaneously, by the state to another state and to the FPLS.

Also, enforcement agencies use the federal income tax return to find out where the noncustodial parent lives and what he or she earns. Under certain conditions, the IRS, working through the State and Federal Child Support Enforcement Agencies, may disclose to the child support office information that income providers submit on IRS Form 1099. This information is a valuable tool to help find a noncustodial parent and determine his or her financial assets. The information may only be used for the purpose of enforcing child support payments.

Information available through Form 1099 includes both earned and unearned income, including wages, earnings on stocks and bonds, interest from bank accounts, unemployment compensation, capital gains, royalties and prizes, and employer and financial institution addresses. A number of small businesses submit 1099 asset information to the IRS, so this can be a good source of information. Any information obtained from the IRS must be verified through a second source, such as an employer or bank, before the CSE agency can use it.

When the caseworker has the current address of the noncustodial parent, he or she will verify the home and work addresses then ask the noncustodial parent to come to the CSE office for an interview. Legal action may be taken.

Even if the father is in the military, the enforcement agency can find him. The FPLS can provide the current duty station of a parent who is in any of the uniformed services.

MARILYN'S STORY

After gathering the information in this section, I went to my sister who had a child from a previous marriage. Marilyn married Jack, moved into a cozy apartment, and began their life as a married couple. Several months passed and they decided to have a child. Nine months later, a healthy baby boy was born. They gave him love and provided for his needs. Then came a bitter divorce with personal items at stake as well as the support of the three year old. Marilyn took custody of her son and got a support order included in her divorce decree. After the divorce, she never saw him again, nor has he seen his son.

Marilyn has never collected child support from him because he cannot be located. She has his SSN but no home address or other pertinent information. She told me that he takes a job and as soon as he is located by child support agencies, he quits that job to find another. This cycle has continued for eight years. Even though there are measures CSE can employ, without a steady job, he can continue to evade the system.

To date, he continues to move from job to job whenever he is located by the CSEA.

NOTES

PHASE TWO

**PATERNITY:
ESTABLISH LEGAL FATHERHOOD
FOR CHILDREN**

Alex and I dated for a period of time and he was the only person I was dating. I had my own company and traveled intensively. I enjoyed returning home from a long trip to hang out with Alex. When I was away, we would have long talks on the phone. I admired Alex and saw longevity with him. We were both ambitious and wanted so much out of life. Our intimacy was special and cherished. I can recall when our son was conceived and when I found out I was pregnant. I told Alex about the pregnancy and for a period of 24 hours, he was the most charming, caring, and concerned person I knew. But he told me that he was not prepared to have a child right then. Still, I knew what my decision was and that no matter what, I was going to have a child. Alex was the father, no confusions and no other possibilities. I had no other sex partners.

Throughout the pregnancy, Alex was distant. He did not want anything to do with the pregnancy. My theory was that his friends turned his excitement into fear and he fled. I endured a great pregnancy with the support of his family in Atlanta. Austin was conceived in December and in April, Alex left to attend school in another city. The distance was great because I did not have to have any confrontations with him. I was relaxed and it was easy sailing with the pregnancy.

When Austin was born and Alex and I had gone our separate ways, I did not want anything at all to do with Alex. I vowed that I would take care of Austin. I wanted Alex to give up all parental rights, visitation rights, and financial obligations. I had watched a movie by Danielle Steele, and in the movie, the biological father had given up all rights to his child. I really meant it when I told him to do the same thing.

My decision was based on his actions. He was very mean and verbally abusive to me. He resented me for deciding to have our son. I resented him for resenting me. I was an independent young female operating my own business, living life to its fullest. I thought I did not need a man to define who I was, who my son would be, or how I would raise him. I was wrong. He defined who his son is because he was a part of him. I realized how selfish my thinking was to ask. He wasn't doing it anyway and I felt threatened. I wanted him far away from me and in turn would keep him far away from his son. I had to separate my feelings about Alex and think about the welfare of our son. Our son needed his father in his life.

I must admit, the most humiliating aspect of my experience with the child support process was when the prosecuting attorney told me that my son and I had to take a paternity test because his father was requesting one. I was flabbergasted and could not believe what I was hearing. The embarrassment was overwhelming. I cried to my girlfriend Allison. He knew that he was the father. He had spent a lot of valuable time with our son, taking care of our son until this point. Did he not believe that Austin was his son? Did he think I had lied to him? My pride was so badly damaged that for days, I could not think about anything else. It was like he was denying his son and wanted to prove that he wasn't the father after all. I hurt for my son and what it would do to him.

The prosecuting attorney arranged with my caseworker a date for my son and me to take the test and for Alex to take the same test in the state in which he lives. She explained the process and how long it would take for the results to return. She told me that once the paternity was established, it would be easier to obtain a support order. That was good news, but nothing was making the thought of taking the paternity test any easier or what it would do to our son. I did not know if this was a game for Alex, but he was playing with his son's life.

I explained to Austin, as simply as I could, what we had to do and what it would prove. On the day of the test, I took him out of school and drove to the testing location, which was in the office where I filed for the support order. After telling him the process, my son asked so eloquently, "Mom, doesn't he know that I am his son and that child support is for me?" Tears gushed out of my eyes and I found myself calling Alex on the cell phone to express my disgust with having to subject our son to this. He said that he knew Austin was his and that his attorney suggested that he asked for the paternity test. I then repeated what our son said to me and told him that he would have to live with his decision for the rest of his life.

The paternity procedure was painless nevertheless. We arrived at the location. There was an outside company that does DNA testing performing the test. The gentleman verified our identity and then opened a package of what looked like a Q-tip, swiped the inside of our jaws and placed the Q-tip in a tube, sealed it, and dismissed us. We went to lunch and have never discussed that day again. Weeks passed and I received a letter with the result of the paternity test. Of course, it said Alex was the father. And I never said anything after that. I was utterly disappointed in Alex's decision and his attempt to justify his decision to take a paternity test by saying his attorney advised him to do so.

Many fathers voluntarily acknowledge paternity. Hospitals must provide fathers the opportunity to acknowledge paternity voluntarily at the time of birth. In a disputed case, father, mother, and child can be required to submit to genetic tests. The genetic test results are highly accurate. States must have procedures that allow paternity to be established up to the child's eighteenth birthday.

When children are born out of wedlock, establishing paternity is a first step for obtaining a child support order. Paternity establishment involves the legal establishment of fatherhood for a child. Paternity can be established by a voluntary acknowledgement signed by both parents, as part of an in-hospital or other acknowledgement program.

Under the Personal Responsibility and Work Opportunity Act of 1996 (PRWORA) an acknowledgment of paternity becomes a finding of paternity unless the man who signed the acknowledgment denies that he is the father within

60 days. If it becomes necessary to seek child support, a finding of paternity creates the basis for a child support order. A support order against the father cannot be established for a child who is born to unmarried parents until paternity has been established.

Paternity establishment provides basic emotional, social, and economic ties between a father and his child. Once paternity is established legally, a child gains legal rights and privileges. Among these may be rights to inheritance, rights to the father's medical and life insurance benefits, and to social security and possibly veterans' benefits. The child also has a chance to develop a relationship with the father, and to develop a sense of identity and connection to the "other half" of his or her family. It may be important for the health of the child for doctors to have knowledge of the father's medical history.

The caseworker will also want to know whether he ever provided any financial support or in any other way acknowledged—through letters or gifts—that the child was his. A picture of the alleged father with the child is helpful, as well as any information from others who could confirm your relationship with him.

Paternity can be determined by administrative procedures which take into account highly accurate tests conducted on blood or tissue samples of the man, mother and child. Genetic test results indicate a probability of paternity and can establish a legal presumption of paternity. These tests have an accuracy range of between 90 and 99 percent. They can exclude a man who is not the biological father and can also show the likelihood of paternity if he is not excluded. Each party in a contested paternity case must submit to genetic tests at the request of either party or the CSE agency.

If the state orders the tests, the state must pay the cost of the testing. If the father is identified by the tests, some states will charge him for their costs. If a party disputes the original test result, he or she can pay for a second genetic test and the state must then obtain additional testing. If the father could be one of several men, each may be required to take a genetic test.

You can apply for child support enforcement services at your local CSE office. If he is willing to sign documents to acknowledge paternity and agree to support, then enforcement can proceed by a wage withholding order. If the man is on a naval ship or lives on a military base abroad and will not acknowledge paternity, it may be necessary to wait until he returns to the United States for blood work to be done. (See more details in the Military Section of this book)

If the accused father fails to respond to a formal complaint properly served upon him, a default judgment can be entered in court. The default judgment establishes paternity. At the same time, a court order for support may be issued. If the parent has disappeared, State and Federal

Parent Locator Services can be called on to help find him. States must give full faith and credit to paternity determinations made by other states in accordance with their laws and regulations.

There are circumstances that custodial parents may deem reasonable to not establish paternity with the father, such as the father is a teenager and does not work or the father is of legal age and does not work. Regardless of age or work status of the father, when the father gets older and starts working, he will be able to support the child. Having paternity established legally, even if the order for support is delayed, means collecting child support will be easier later. There are, however, few situations when it is not in children's best interest to have paternity established. Instances in which the father is a threat to the family and causes bodily injury to children are justifiable to not establish paternity.

However, knowing their father and having his emotional and financial support is very important to children. Also, remember, the child's father has the right to request genetic testing to prove that he is the father and he can then establish the legal right to a relationship with his child. If you are worried about your or the child's safety if you try to establish paternity, or if you need to be in a cash assistance program, you may talk with your caseworker about showing "good cause" for not naming the father.

NOTES

NOTES

NONCUSTODIAL PARENTS INVOLVEMENT IN CHILDREN LIVES

From the time Alex saw Austin, he has always played a vital role in Austin's life. He picked up Austin and would drive him back to college with him. I lived in Atlanta, GA, and he went to school in a nearby town. He was very proud of his son and spent any time with him that he could. I cherished those moments.

Even when Alex moved out-of-state he would visit Atlanta to see his son or I would fly Austin to visit his father. Austin would stay with his father several months at a time. This went on for several years. The bond that was established because Alex was physically in his life has no monetary value; it was priceless. The bond between them both was established way before I filed for child support.

Austin always has a great time visiting his father. His aunts, grandparents, and other relatives on his father's side love him, and his younger sister and brother anticipate each visit. They look forward to each visit from Austin and to spending quality time with him. We have worked out that Austin spends the summers with him and Thanksgiving or Christmas. Most of the time he spends both there. I have always fostered this relationship and vowed to myself to separate the financial responsibility from visitation rights. Even when Alex was not paying child support, I would still allow Austin to visit him. I had to bite my tongue many times or had to remind myself what was important to Austin. Taking away quality time with his father was not going to make his father pay. It was only going to hurt Austin.

Research shows that children benefit from positive relationships not only with their mothers but also with their fathers. Higher levels of father's involvement in activities with their children, such as eating meals together, going on outings, and helping with homework, are associated with fewer behavior problems, higher levels of sociability, and a higher level of school performance among children and adolescents.

Fathers' involvement in children's schooling, such as volunteering at school and attending school meetings, parent-teacher conferences and class events, is associated with higher grades, greater school enjoyment, and lower chances of suspension or expulsion from school.

The father-child relationship affects daughters as well as sons. Girls who live with both their mother and father do better academically. In addition, they are less likely to engage in sexual activity at an early age and in the use of alcohol or drugs.

Keeping fathers connected to their children and increasing fathers' involvement in the lives of their children poses significant challenges for our nation; high rates of divorce, non-marital child bearing, and the financial and emotional stresses of raising children with severe special health care needs increase the risk that fathers will be less involved in their children's lives.

As more families have two parents working outside

the home, fathers need support in the work place to find ways to balance work and family obligations and provide children with the level of child-parent involvement and supervision needed for their healthy growth and development.

While government cannot make good fathers, it can support efforts to help men become the best fathers they can be.

THE ROLE I WANT THE OTHER PARENT TO PLAY IN THE LIFE OF MY CHILD.

NOTES

PHASE THREE

OBLIGATION: ESTABLISH THE SUPPORT ORDER

I had successfully provided my caseworker with all the information to secure an order for my son, including establishing paternity. I began the process in September of 1998. Going through the phases, I could not believe how long it took to just establish the support order. Alex used the law to his advantage. Whenever we would have a court date to establish the support order, he would ask for a continuance. This is legal and allows the court to delay the case to a later date. Believe it or not, he asked for seven continuances, which delayed the case for over one year. I'll give it to him, he was smart. But the system was smarter; it only delayed the inevitable, that a support order would be established. And to my benefit, I received back payment for that period of time.

I had contacted the CSE office in his state to learn who the caseworker was and who the prosecuting attorney was. I developed a relationship with both but moreso with the prosecuting attorney. I became so knowledgeable that I thought I could assist others in their process. This is where the idea to write a book was born.

I remember talking to my caseworker occasionally by phone to update him on the case and frequently with the prosecuting attorney. I don't know how standard that was, but I had to know what was going on at all times. I had taken a good time out of my daily life to devote to this phase of the process and I had to maintain my patience because every time a court date was established it would be changed because of Alex's attorney's strategy.

When it was time to arrange for the amount that Alex would pay, I had to study both states' laws. Some states do not recognize back child support and both of the states I was dealing with had the same laws towards back child support. I had to think fast and think smart. We had established, by verbal agreement, that he would pay a certain amount in the past. The checks for child support payments that he sent to me were evidence that child support was established. This allowed for me to establish a case for back child support and to include the back payments in the child support order that we were establishing.

I spent over two years, from filing for child support to establishing a support order working with the caseworkers and the prosecuting attorney, to prove my case. In spite of my dedication, I experienced many emotions, from defeat to triumph, from hurt and pain to total satisfaction.

Establishing a support order depends on how much success you and your caseworker or lawyer have in several critical areas, such as locating the noncustodial parent, if necessary, identifying what he or she can pay, and determining the financial needs of the child.

States are required to have child support guidelines available to all people who set child support amounts. Most states' guidelines consider the needs of the child, other dependents, and the ability of the parents to pay. States must use the guidelines unless they can be shown to be inappropriate in a particular case.

States today have arrangements for establishing the support order by an administrative procedure or other expedited legal procedure. The hearing may be conducted by a master, or a referee of the court, or by an administrative hearings officer. An agreement made between the parents, based on the appropriate child support guidelines and approved by this kind of agency, generally has the same effect as one established in court. It is legally binding on the parties concerned.

The agreement that the parents make should provide for the child's present and future well-being. It may be useful to discuss these issues together if you can, or with a mediator or family counselor. You may call your Child Support Enforcement (CSE) office to find out about your state's guidelines.

The caseworker will make every possible effort to identify the parent's employment, any property owned, and any other sources of income or assets. This information must be verified before the support order is final. Under certain situations, the IRS may provide financial information about the parent's earned and unearned income, such as interest payments and unemployment compensation. The state CSE agency now has access to financial institution data, such as bank accounts, and credit bureau data, which may provide information about employers and/or assets.

If parents can cooperate and agree on the amount of support and how often the payment will be received, all the better. You can get help from a lawyer, mediator or family counselor. The court's sole interest in your agreement is to see that it is fair to all parties, that the welfare of the children is protected, and that the agreement conforms with the guidelines.

In some states' guidelines, both parents' earnings are considered in setting the amount of the support order. In other states' guidelines, only the noncustodial parent's earnings area considered. Check with your CSE office. Laws vary from state to state, but parents who can work out a fair support agreement between them will have a better chance of having their wishes recognized in court.

Some states have guideline formulas that take joint custody into account. The same factors would apply: state guidelines, each parent's ability to pay, and the needs of the child.

CSE offices reviews child support orders every three years if either parent requests such a review. Ask your caseworker for information about reviewing and, if appropriate, modifying your child support order. States can adjust child support orders using child support guidelines, to take into account cost of living adjustments, or automated methods determined by the state.

If you go to your CSE office for a modification of your order, the income and assets of the noncustodial parent, financial situation, and any special needs of the child will need to be determined. If appropriate, the agency can then seek a legal modification.

The amount that can be withheld from an employee's disposable wages is limited by the Federal Consumer Credit Protection Act (FCCPA) to 50 percent of disposable earnings if an obligated parent has a second family and 60 percent if there is no second family. These limits are each increased by 5 percent (to 55% and 65%) if payments are in arrears for a period equal to 12 weeks or more. State law may further limit the amount that can be taken from a wage earner's paycheck.

In some states, the judge may grant the noncustodial parent a decrease in the obligation based on guidelines for child support. You should be notified beforehand and given an opportunity to contest the proposed change. Other factors that could lower the support order include steady employment of the child or poor health or decreased earning ability of the noncustodial parent.

State guidelines may indicate how child support is to be shared when there is more than one support order. If the noncustodial parent income will not provide for both orders, the amount of support for your children may be reduced, but you will receive a share of the support collected. For orders enforced by wage withholding, states must have a formula for sharing the available income among the support orders. Ask your caseworker for more information.

The CSE agency must petition the court to include

medical support in any order for child support when employment-related or other group health insurance is available to the noncustodial parent at a reasonable cost. Court orders can also be modified to include health care coverage.

If you are not receiving cash assistance or Medicaid, the CSE agency will help you enforce a medical support order if you want it. If you do not want its help, you may decline it. For people on cash assistance, or Medicaid, the CSE agency must order the noncustodial parent to provide health insurance if it is available.

Federal law requires states to have laws that should make medical support enforcement easier. For example, insurers can no longer refuse to enroll a child in a health care plan because the parents were not married or because the child does not live in the same household as the enrolled parent. The law also created a tool that child support agencies will be able to use to establish and enforce medical support when the noncustodial parent participates in a group health plan but does not enroll the child.

This law provides that custodial parents can obtain information about coverage directly from an insurer, submit claims directly to the insurer, and be reimbursed directly by an insurer. For specific information about these laws in your state, contact the CSE office.

Past due support may accumulate while the father is in

jail. But unless he has other assets, such as property or any income such as wages from a work-release program, it is unlikely that support can be collected while he is in jail. Depending on state law, your support order may be modified so that payment is deferred until he is released and working.

If your case does not meet the state's standards for review, either because the order has been reviewed within three years or the change in income is smaller than would merit an adjustment under state standards, you may still be able to petition the courts for a hearing. In this case, it may be helpful to have the services of an attorney. Your local legal aid society may be able to provide low-cost counsel to parents who cannot afford a private attorney. Also, a number of states have information about how to handle your case pro se (a legal term for representing yourself) to have the courts determine if your support obligation should be changed. Contact your local CSE office or the court.

If and when child support enforcement becomes an issue, it is necessary to have a legal order for child support spelling out the amount of the obligation and how it is to be paid. Data from the United States Census Bureau show that, of the over 11 million families with a parent living elsewhere, only 56 percent have legally binding support orders.

NOTES

PHASE FOUR

ENFORCEMENT: COLLECT CHILD SUPPORT PAYMENTS

WHEN THE NON-CUSTODIAL PARENT DOES NOT PAY

I had successfully obtained a support order. What next? Just because you have a support order does not automatically mean that the noncustodial parent will pay. Establishing a support order is a crucial step in the process. However, the key is collecting your child support payments on a regular basis. This step can be sometimes frustrating and cause many custodial parents to give up on the system.

My child support payment was set up for automatic deposit in my checking account. Every time Alex got paid, child support payment was deducted from his paycheck and would automatically go to the payment center in his state, then be transferred to my state and then deposited into my account. However, after having a support order established, I experienced a period of time when Alex did not pay according to the support order.

I received a phone call as Austin and I were out eating at Austin's favorite restaurant the day before he would fly to visit his father for the summer. I answered my cell phone, expecting further arrangements for Austin's flight. However, I was amazed with what he had told me. He told me that he was on administrative leave and that he would not be able to pay child support. I moved the phone away from my ear and looked at it in astonishment. I was in such shock that I said okay and got off the phone to avoid confrontation in front of Austin. I did not know what to say or what to do.

How can I make him pay when he did not have a job?

I called my girlfriend who knew Alex very well. Lori encouraged me to be patient and not to do or say anything irrational. I took her advice and did further research on when a noncustodial parent does not pay according to the support order. I did not prevent Austin from getting on the flight the next day. Child support payments stopped, and I did nothing. I did not have to do anything because according to the support order, when he did not pay, he falls into arrears and he is still responsible for the payment.

Under the law, by establishing a support order and defining the terms by which a support order should be paid, Alex was liable. I learned this from my research on child support enforcement. During the several months that he was jobless, he did not pay child support. When he did resume working, payments started back. And for the time that he did not pay, he was still responsible.

I received a call from him asking me to waive the payment for the time that he was out of work.

After a period of time, the CSE office will use several different methods to collect past due child support. In our instance, his caseworker called me to negotiate a payback amount. Alex had told him that I had agreed to accept a lower amount than was owed. Alex did ask me to waive the total amount or accept a lower amount but, I had not agreed to it at the time. Later, I did however negotiate a lower payback amount.

What most noncustodial parents do not realize is that child support is one of the first obligations they are required to pay monthly. Nothing can exempt them from paying child support; not being unemployed, not a bankruptcy, not even imprisonment. The Child Support Recovery Act of 1992 makes it a federal crime to willfully fail to pay a past due child support obligation for a child living in another state. The past due child support obligation must be either greater than $5,000 or must have remained unpaid for more than one year in order to establish willfulness. The United States Attorney's Office must prove that the noncustodial parent knew about the obligation, was financially able to meet it at the time it was due, and intentionally did not pay it.

Recently, I called Alex to get the medical insurance information for Austin. I wanted to get a jump on getting his physical for the year. He told me that he no longer had insurance because he is no longer employed. He said the insurance was good up until the end of the month. He said that he would not be able to pay child support and wanted to work out a settlement for the back child support that was owed. I thought, not again. Did he not learn the first time around? Didn't he know that this was something he could not just put aside?

It's been several months now, and he has not taken any actions in paying child support and hasn't called to make any payment arrangement. Just like before, I am awaiting the phone call from the caseworker in his state or from him asking me to come to some type of agreement for him to pay back what he has not paid. The amount I receive monthly is not substantial, considering his salary. I never asked for an upward modification even though I knew his salary doubled from the time when an order was established. Now, I feel slighted because he is not paying. That's is why the Federal government places a heavy burden on enforcing support orders.

I mentioned before that this book is for those who are contemplating, going through or have already gone through the process-because even though you have established a support order, there are times when the noncustodial will not pay. This action from the noncustodial parent cannot be predicted or anticipated. What's important to note is that once you have a support order, the noncustodial is obligated to pay.

The CSE program effort is to collect support from parents who are legally obligated to pay. While programs vary from state to state, services are available to all parents who need them. The Child Support Recovery Act adds another remedy to the variety of enforcement tools available to collect child support payments. When a noncustodial parent does not pay according to the support order, he/she is defying the child support court order. This action is against the laws established under The Child Support Recovery Act. And a noncustodial parent can face severe punishment.

There are considerable numbers of noncustodial

parent who avoid paying support for some reason. Some are deadbeat dads who avoid the system. Others face financial crises that prevent them from paying. Whatever the circumstances may be, the bottom line is once a support order is established, the noncustodial parent must pay according to the terms of the support order. Failure to do so may result in imprisonment and garnishment of wages. There are other remedies to make a noncustodial parent pay. These remedies are built into the child support system that strengthens families to be self-sufficient. Cases considered suitable for prosecution are those in which all reasonably available remedies have been exhausted. Among such cases priority is given:

(1) where there is a pattern of moving from state to state to avoid payment;
(2) where there is a pattern of deception (e.g., use of false name or Social Security Number);
(3) where there is failure to make support payments after being held in contempt of court; and
(4) where failure to make support payments is connected to some other federal offense such as bankruptcy fraud.

Generally, cases that are accepted for possible Federal prosecution will be those that have proved unenforceable using the tools that are available through the CSE program. Someone applying directly to the U.S. Attorney's Office may be referred to the state or local CSE office for review of his/her case to ensure that other appropriate remedies have been tried.

When the CSE office has screened and referred the case, the United States Attorney can be reasonably assured of receiving significant information about the case and that the civil and state criminal remedies are exhausted.

Failure to pay support for a child living in another state is punishable by up to six months imprisonment and/or a fine. Second and subsequent violations are punishable by two years imprisonment and/or a fine.

Custodial parents can help their state CSE office and the United States Attorney by providing the noncustodial parent's name, SSN, address, date and place of birth, home/ work telephone numbers, past employment history, and assets. It is also helpful for the custodial parent to provide the divorce/separation agreement, child and/or spousal support order, complete record of any child support payments received, and history of actions taken to enforce the obligation.

The Federal Tax Refund Offset Program collects past due payments of child support from the tax refunds of parents who have been ordered to pay child support. The program is a cooperative effort among the Internal Revenue Service (IRS), Federal Office of Child Support Enforcement (OCSE), and State Child Support Enforcement (CSE) agencies.

Each year, CSE agencies submit to the IRS the names, Social Security Numbers, and the amount of past due child support of people who are behind in their payments. When the IRS processes tax returns, it identifies returns of those who owe child support. If a refund is due, all or part of the refund is collected to offset past due child support payments.

If the parent who owes child support is due a refund, the amount of past due payments is taken out of the refund check and sent to OCSE and then to the state which submitted the case. In Aid to Families with Dependent Children (AFDC) cases, the state keeps the money to help pay for AFDC payments. In non-AFDC cases, the state gives the money directly to the parent and child. If the case is both AFDC and non- AFDC, the AFDC arrearages are paid first.

Cases eligible for a tax refund offset are those cases that have delinquent child support orders. If the child support order includes an award for spousal support, the tax refund may also cover past due spousal support. For cases receiving AFDC, the amount owed by noncustodial parents must be at least $150; in non-AFDC cases, the amount must be at least $500. In all cases, the parent who owes support must be at least three months behind in child support payments.

The Child Support Enforcement Agency or your private attorney will need the noncustodial parent's name, SSN, and the amount of past due child to submit a case to IRS. The state will also need to know the noncustodial parent's address so that he/she can be notified that his/her name is being submitted to the IRS to offset the tax refund for past due child support. This offset notification provides an opportunity for the noncustodial parent to pay past due child support or disagree with the amount of money the CSE agency says is owed.

States are required to submit all cases (both AFDC and non-AFDC) that meet the criteria for submittal. The state or local CSE agency may notify custodial parents that their case has been submitted for tax refund offset. Some states have a charge for non-AFDC cases; others do not. States cannot charge more than $25 for this service.

IRS processes tax returns beginning in February through December. It takes three to five weeks from the time the IRS processes the return until the money is sent to the state. In non-AFDC cases, the state may hold the money for up to six months if it involves a joint return.

Regardless of where a parent who owes support lives in the United States, the tax return will be processed by the IRS through the same system. Tax returns are filed only once a year, so timing is very important. Plan on contacting the state or local CSE agency as soon as possible to find out their deadline for submitting the names and SSNs of parents who owe child support. Then, the agency will determine whether the case should be submitted.

I did not know how effective this process was until

I received a credit into my checking account for twice the amount of support I expected to receive. Alex was the one that told me in a conversation several weeks later that his tax return was offset to pay me what he owed in back support payment. I did not have to contact my caseworker; once the noncustodial parent is behind, the system knows it and pursues the appropriate measures to collect the unpaid amount.

ANGELA STORY

My girlfriend Angela had a child with an NFL player, her college sweetheart. After he entered the NFL, the relationship went sour. Angela was left to raise little Brianna alone. She got wise and filled for a support order. She was awarded a support order in excess of $2,000.00 monthly. This amount allowed Angela to provide a great life for Brianna. She participated in many activities and most of all, each summer she would go away to attend an overnight camp for several weeks. However, with trades and the constant moving of professional athletes, child support payment became irregular and it became hard for Angela to keep up with the lifestyle that she had provided for Brianna. Child support arrearage reached in the thirty thousand dollar range. She hired a private attorney to pursue arrearage. Her child's father eventually was released from his team, which made matters even more complicated. This athlete had married and had other children, along with a fleet of cars, a beautiful house and vehicles for his mother and siblings. According to records, he had paid tithes over $50,000 for the year and he had hired an architect to whom he paid $120,000 in cash to design a new house. All this was happening without him paying child support. Angela got very wise, gathered all the information, presented it to the attorney and strengthened her case against her child's father.

I remember going to court with Angela, watching him lie about his financial predicament and payment to accommodate his current lifestyle. When it was Angela's turn on the stand, she provided information that was documented. The judge denied downward modification and demanded that he pay her the arrearage owed in a timely manner. By knowing the law and by my having gone through the process, she was encouraged to pursue what was legally hers. The Child Support Recovery Act protected her.

NOTES

HOW SUPPORT PAYMENTS ARE COLLECTED

A main objective of the Child Support Enforcement Program is to make sure that child support payments are made regularly and in the correct amount. While many noncustodial parents are involved in their children's lives and are willing to pay child support, lapses of payment do occur. When they do, a family's budget can be quickly and seriously threatened, and the anxiety the custodial parent feels can easily disrupt the family's life. Furthermore, child support enforcement provides hope as well as support to America's children.

Child support payments are collected through various methods, such as income withholding, unemployment compensation interception, and state or federal income tax refund offsets. The most successful way to collect child support is by direct withholding from the obligated parent's paycheck. Most child support orders require the employer to withhold the money that is ordered for child support and send it to the CSE office.

For this reason, Congress decided that immediate wage withholding should be included in all child support orders. (States must also apply withholding to sources of income other than wages.) If the noncustodial parent has a regular job, wage withholding for child support can be treated like other forms of payroll deduction—income tax, social security, union dues, or any other required payment. For child support orders issued or modified through state CSE programs, immediate wage withholding began November

1, 1990. Immediate wage withholding began January 1, 1994 for all initial orders that are not established through the CSE program. The law allows for an exception to immediate wage withholding if the court (or administrative process) finds good cause or if both parents agree to an alternative arrangement. In these cases, an arrearage equal to one month's payment will trigger withholding.

If payments are skipped or stopped entirely, especially if the noncustodial parent is self-employed, works for cash or commissions, changes employment, or moves frequently, the CSE office will try to enforce the support order through other means. Subject to due process safeguards, states have laws which allow them to use enforcement techniques such as state and federal income tax offset, liens on real or personal property owned by the debtor, orders to withhold and deliver property that may satisfy the debt, or a seizure and sale of property with the proceeds from the sale applied to the support debt. The CSE office can use these methods without directly involving the courts.

When the other parent does not work regularly and keeps falling behind in child support payments, there are other ways the court can establish regular payment, such as property liens and attachments. In certain cases, federal law also authorizes that the parent be required to post security, bond, or other guarantee to cover support obligations. These may be in the form of money or property.

If the noncustodial parent refuses to pay child support

but owns a good deal of property in the county, a lien can be issued on the property. A lien on property does not by itself result in the immediate collection of any money. It only prevents the owner from selling, transferring, or borrowing against the property until the child support debt is paid. However, the presence of a property lien may encourage the noncustodial parent to pay the past due child support in order to retain clear title to the property. States are now required to give full faith and credit to liens issued by another state. Most states will not put a lien on a primary residence or attach property that a person needs to make a living. Talk to your caseworker about what kinds of property are available for liens and attachment in your state.

Also, it is possible to collect the support payments from personal property if the noncustodial parent has not paid for a period of time. Under some states' laws, the enforcement official can issue an order to withhold and deliver. The order is sent to the person, company, or institution that is holding property belonging to the debtor, such as a bank account, investments, or personal property. The holder of the property must deliver it either to the enforcement agency or court that issued the support order. Some states permit the property to be attached or seized and sold to pay the debt. Some states require noncustodial parents with a poor payment history to pledge property as a guarantee of payment. Non-payment results in forfeiture of the property.

If you are working with an attorney, your attorney can

work with the child support program. For best results, they should coordinate their efforts to prevent duplication of services and conflicting enforcement decisions. The attorney can request wage withholding for child support payments. You can collect support through wage withholding if you use a private attorney rather than the CSE office. States must also apply withholding to other kinds of income in addition to wages, such as bonuses, commissions, retirement, rental or interest income.

If you have already established a support order through a divorce decree or other means, the wage withholding can be applied to existing child support order. You can apply for the wage withholding through your local CSE office or your attorney. Though there are limits on how much of a person's check can be withheld, wage withholding can be used for both ongoing support and arrearages.

When the noncustodial parent lives in another state, the state must recognize the wage withholding orders and continue the wage withholding as ordered, without regard to where the noncustodial parent or the custodial parent and children live.

Regardless of any conditions or circumstances causing the collection of child support using the wage withholding, under Federal law, an employer must withhold the support if ordered to or if the noncustodial parent requests it.

Another condition that is under scrutiny for enforcing

child support order is the noncustodial parent working irregularly and being paid in cash; wage withholding won't work for you. Automatic billing, telephone reminders, and delinquency notices from your CSE office might convince him to make regular payments. Other techniques, such as property attachment, credit bureau reporting, tax refund offset, and liens might work for the arrearages. The Personal Responsibility and Work Opportunity Reconciliation Act of 1996 (PRWORA) requires states to enact legislation to allow suspending or revoking drivers, professional, occupational and recreational licenses if an arrearage develops. If none of these is successful, your enforcement office can take the case to court for stronger enforcement methods.

Some noncustodial parents try to hide earnings when they are self-employed. If the noncustodial parent is self employed, the CSE office can find out how much is earned and determine how they can collect the money. The CSE office has access to information from the Internal Revenue Service to determine income and assets. This information will help to set the support order amount.

Cases involving self-employed noncustodial parents can be the most challenging to work and often take more time and effort. If it is not possible to arrange for an allotment or withholding, it may be possible to secure liens on his or her payments from regular clients or to garnish his or her bank account. If a business depends on having a license, the owner/parent may make arrangements to pay rather than risk losing his or her license. Knowing that arrearages will be reported to a credit bureau may give the owner/parent a strong incentive to comply with the order. Provide your caseworker with as much information as you can about the business and his or her clients.

Members of the military are subject to the same wage withholding requirements as other public or private employees. Federal garnishment procedures should be used in most instances, although use of military involuntary allotments is sometimes more appropriate. If a service member is not meeting a support obligation, a wage withholding order can be sent to the Defense Finance and Accounting Service (DFAS) Center in Cleveland, Ohio. (See more details in the Military section of this book.)

It is possible to garnish the income of retired members of the military. With the assistance of your caseworker or lawyer, you can get a garnishment order from the court and send it with a certified copy of your child support order to DFAS. Your local enforcement office can tell you the exact procedures and follow through on your behalf.

No one is exempt from paying child support. Even Federal employees are subject to wage withholding, and there is a central payment office for each Department. Moves within the Department should not affect a wage withholding order. If you do not have a formal support order, ask a child support office or an attorney about establishing one. If you have a child support order, your CSE office or attorney can help you to secure payments by wage withholding. If the noncustodial parent has moved to a different department, the Federal Parent Locator Service (FPLS) can provide the new location.

Under Federal law, all states with state income tax must offset state income tax refunds for past due support owed to families and to states for cash assistance they have provided. The state must notify the noncustodial parent in advance of taking the action. The notice specifies the amount owed in arrears and the amount to be offset. It also tells whom to contact if the person wants to contest the offset. States can request an offset of federal income tax refunds for past due support of over $500 owed on behalf of minor children not receiving cash assistance as well as over $150 owed to states that have provided assistance.

Your caseworker may be able to make a request for use of the IRS "full collection" technique. Under certain conditions, the Internal Revenue Service can attach a parent's income and other assets for child support payments. The CSE agency can submit the request when the amount owed is over $750 and there is good evidence that the obligated parent has assets that can be tapped for collection. Contact your caseworker for more information.

Unemployment compensation and other state and federal benefits can be tapped for child support. Ask your caseworker about the procedures, and make sure you tell your caseworker immediately if you learn about changes in the noncustodial parent's employment situation.

If you are owed past due child support, the enforcement agency can try to collect the arrearage. If the support was owed before the CSE office became involved in your case, the CSE office will have to verify the amount owed and may have to present the documentation to a court before it can start collection procedures. While it is doing this, the agency can try to collect support payments for current months. By federal law, the CSE office must periodically report the amount of past-due child support to credit reporting agencies. Consult your caseworker for more information.

Child support payments generally cannot be discharged in bankruptcy. This means that the parent who owed child support cannot escape this duty by filing for bankruptcy. As of October 1994, bankruptcies do not act as a stay, or hold, on actions to establish paternity or to establish or modify child support obligations. The relationship between child support and bankruptcy is complex, and you may need the help of someone familiar with bankruptcy law. Ask your caseworker how the CSE office can help.

Courts generally will not allow gifts to a child to take the place of child support and require that child support payments are carried out as ordered by the child support agreement. In some cases, if the voluntary payment is larger than a normal gift would be, a court may decide to credit the payment as a child support payment.

State and local offices are responsible for enforcing

child support orders. The federal government tries to make sure that states use appropriate enforcement techniques. It pays much of the cost of the program, issues policies, offers technical assistance, and reviews state programs for compliance with federal requirements.

If your caseworker and state CSE office have had no response to their requests for enforcement in another jurisdiction, it is possible for the case to be heard by a federal court. This is not done often, and the decision to use a federal court will be made by the federal Regional Office of Child Support Enforcement at the request of your caseworker and the state enforcement office. If you are not satisfied with the services you are receiving in your local CSE office, you may ask your state CSE agency for help. State agency addresses are listed at the end of the handbook.

State statutes of limitations determine how long the CSE office can try to collect on a child support debt. Within this period, the CSE office is required by federal law to collect verified back support.

A well-written child support order should provide for continued support if the noncustodial parent should die. The child support payments should be defined as a claim against his or her estate. The children can also be named as beneficiaries in the noncustodial parent's life insurance policy or will.

The success you have in obtaining regular, adequate, and full child support payments depends to a great extent on how well you can make the child support enforcement system work for you. At the same time, it is important to remember that not all the solutions to your child support problems are within your control. The legal rights and welfare of all parties must be carefully guarded, and sometimes laws that protect the rights of one parent seem unfair to the other.

Knowledge is power. The more you know about child support enforcement procedures where you and the noncustodial parent live, the better you will be able to exercise your rights and responsibilities under the law and the more successful you will be in obtaining the support that rightfully belongs to your children. As you proceed with your enforcement case, it is a good idea to keep a written account of the actions taken and the outcomes of those actions. Do not hesitate to ask questions and make suggestions to your enforcement caseworker. If you are not satisfied with the actions taken on your behalf, you have recourse with the head of the local CSE office as well as to the director of the State Child Support Enforcement Agency. Keep in mind that it is always best to communicate the problem in writing.

An informed parent can make the child support enforcement system work. This, together with improvements that state enforcement programs, legislatures, and the courts are making, can benefit millions of parents and their children.

NOTES

CHILD SUPPORT ENFORCEMENT FOR NATIVE AMERICAN CHILDREN

The Native American Child Support Program in the federal Office of Child Support Enforcement has been consulting with the tribes and Native American organizations to ensure that Native American children receive the child support to which they are entitled. New provisions in the Personal Responsibility and Work Opportunities Reconciliation Act (PRWORA) provide more options to achieve this goal.

American Indian tribes or tribal organizations will be eligible to apply for grants to operate full or partial child support enforcement programs. The projects must meet child support enforcement criteria that were issued through regulations in mid-1998. Formal consultation is planned for the proposed rules.

Native American reservations are governed by tribal laws that may differ from those of the states, just as laws differ from state to state. The differences, and the various types of state and tribal court systems, sometimes make it difficult to enforce child support orders or to locate absent parents on reservations.

However, some states and tribes have entered into cooperative agreements to facilitate obtaining child support for Native American children. If tribes do not operate child support enforcement programs, it is expected that more tribes and states will enter into Cooperative Agreements to work together to carry out their child support responsibilities.

In the interim, tribal and state child support staffs will continue to pursue all available means to assist Native American children to receive support. What works best, and barriers encountered, will be shared. This will assist tribes in deciding how best to meet child support enforcement requirements through tribal programs or cooperative agreements with states.

It may be difficult to establish or enforce a child support order when the non-custodial parent lives and works on an Indian reservation if the tribe does not have an agreement with a state to establish or enforce each other's child support orders. When a tribe has an agreement with a state CSE agency to establish paternity, locate absent parents, or enforce or modify child support orders, state and local CSE staff and the tribal courts work together to obtain the child support for Native American children.

State CSE agencies and OCSE are currently working with a number of tribes to develop cooperative agreements to solve the complex problems of obtaining child support. Talk with your state or local CSE office about the specific situation and how it can help. Be sure to provide any information about any assets off the Reservation that the noncustodial parent may have.

If your caseworker has not been able to secure child support, check with the tribal leaders to see if there are any provisions established by the tribe for supporting tribal children. Your children may be eligible to receive special services (health, education, general assistance payments, etc.), or some other kind of specialized assistance.

If the noncustodial parent does not fall under the jurisdiction of the tribal court, seek assistance for your child through the tribe if you live on the reservation. If the tribe does not have an agreement with the state, also work directly with the IV-D office in the state, or local, OCSE office to locate the father and establish a child support order.

CHILD SUPPORT ENFORCEMENT AND MILITARY PERSONNEL

TRACEY'S STORY

My girlfriend Tracey was introduced to a guy in the military and fell head over heels with him. They had a telephone courtship for several months. Tracey traveled to where he was stationed for the weekend and had a great time. However, several weeks later, Tracey told me she was pregnant. She did not know how to tell the father and when she did, the worst happened. He denied that he was the father and had nothing else to do with Tracey. Tracey was devastated and alone. I told Tracey to be patient and wait until the day her child was born. She handled the situation very calmly and waited until the day little Christopher was born.

Immediately after the birth of her son, she contacted her district councilperson and wrote a letter explaining her situation. Tracey also contacted the base at which her son's father was stationed and received information from them as to their procedure. She followed the steps that were suggested to her. I lost contact with Tracey for a period of time. When I did see her again, she told me that Christopher was with his dad for the weekend and she had successfully established a support order.

Through Tracey, I learned at least three helpful hints for dealing with the military on civil matters such as child support enforcement. First, ask for help; do not insist on it. Invoking your civilian authority and making demands will often meet resistance. Respect is significant in all military matters. If you show respect for both military personnel and their mission, they will generally show you and your mission the same level of respect.

Second, be prepared to recognize that there are some valid limitations on the military's abilities to respond to your requests. To illustrate, some military information-- such as ship schedules and the dates or locations of military exercises--is routinely classified and cannot be revealed. National security does require some secrecy. Nonetheless, there are well-established ways that you can ask for and can expect to receive the military's help in communicating with any member of any active unit.

Third, use the military command structure to your advantage. Contact the service member first. Then, if necessary, contact the service member's commander or the commander's representative. If you still do not get an acceptable response, then contact the commander's superior and make sure you highlight all your previous attempts to use other points of contact. You will frequently find superiors who will push to resolve personal matters like child support before they interfere with military duties.

In summary, neither Federal law nor military regulations provide military personnel with any permanent protections from U.S. or foreign courts proceedings to establish paternity and child support obligations.

The Soldiers' and Sailors' Civil Relief Act (SSCRA) does provide for temporary stays of proceedings and for re-opening judgments under certain circumstances. However, in all other important respects, child support cases involving military personnel can be handled the same way as civilian cases.

•   To locate military personnel on active duty either in the U.S. or overseas, you will need the person's full name and Social Security Number.

•   It is usually easier and more productive to use the military address (rather than the home address) of military personnel.

•   If your state law permits, use the U.S. mail, which includes all APO and FPO addresses, for service of process and obtaining evidence from military personnel.

•   The U.S. has treaties with some of the nations where military personnel are stationed. These treaties may permit you to work with foreign offices to pursue child support even when the absent parent is overseas.

•   Establishing paternity is a civilian matter, and the military would usually prefer not to be directly involved.

•   Child support obligations should be determined based on total military compensation, often including some tax-free and/or in-kind benefits.

•   Involuntary allotments are typically better than garnishments or wage assignments for collection of child support obligations from military personnel.

•   You can avoid some problems with the SSCRA if you use administrative processes rather than judicial proceedings whenever possible.

        If you have any further questions regarding child support enforcement and military personnel, visit our website or write to Angel Eyes Publishing Co. for Child Support Enforcement and Military Personnel pamphlet. (See Appendix Two.)

NOTES

UNDERSTANDING THE CHILD SUPPORT SYSTEM

GOVERNMENT INTERVENTION

I omitted the legal section of this book but have it available on the website for anyone interested in knowing their legal rights. The information is full of legal jargon and reads like a law book. It is provided for you to know your rights as a citizen and, moreso as a parent collecting the child support that is due to you. These laws were established to protect custodial parents against the disruption of families when one parent is no longer a constant in the child's' life. These laws are varied and consist of guidelines and directions to overcome any situation that may arise in child support enforcement. Nothing is fool proof. Many noncustodial parents find ways to evade and circumvent the system. Some are successful, while others are punished by the establishment of laws to enforce child support payments.

The government on all levels, federal/state/local has worked to making child support enforcement realistic for families. Regardless of your circumstances, the laws are made to protect you as custodial parent and provide you with the financial means to being self-sufficient. Some of the laws are mentioned in this book while others were not. Please, spend time on the website looking over the laws which were made to protect you, both the custodial and noncustodial parent. (See Appendix Three.)

CHILD SUPPORT INITIATIVES

I had a conversation with a friend who is a noncustodial father. I informed him that I was writing a book about child support, and I began to explain the concept of the book to him. He politely interrupted me and said that he was a victim of the child support system and all they do is punish noncustodial parents and treat them like prisoners. In spite of his rough relationship with his ex-wife and his 14-year-old son living in another state, he was one of the fathers that voluntarily accepted paternity and sent the mother $600 every month.

After receiving hostile interactions from his ex-wife, he went to the child support office and as he said, "put himself of child support." I thought *Why didn't my son's father do the same thing?* He continued to say that the system was against the noncustodial father. I informed him that child support was established to provide financial assistance to the child and household of a child when one parent is no longer there.

He had not seen his son in many months. He told me that he had just taken a trip to see his son but the mother would not allow him; they had apparently gotten into another argument. I explained that child support does not enforce visitation; however, they are working on programs that coincide with child support to encourage noncustodial fathers to actively participate in their children's lives. I then conveyed to him that the system was designed to strengthen families, not to take them apart.

I enlightened him that even though his ex-wife has been resistant his seeing his son, there are actions that he could take for him to establish an ongoing relationship with his son through the Child Support Enforcement Office where the case was established and enforced. If this story sounds familiar, I have mentioned Matthew before in my book and this is how our conversation about child support initiated.

The Federal Office of Child Support Enforcement (OCSE) supports various programs and initiatives that support the location of participants in child support cases,collection of child support payments, enforcement of child support orders, communication between states, and online profile information regarding how counties, states, regions, and international offices operate.

IMPROVEMENTS TO CHILD SUPPORT ENFORCEMENT ENACTED UNDER WELFARE REFORM

The 1996 welfare reform law that created the TANF program also included the most extensive child support reforms ever. The changes benefit not only families receiving cash assistance but also other families owed child support. Under the law, each state must operate a child support enforcement program meeting federal requirements in order to be eligible for TANF block grants. Provisions in the law include:

National new hire reporting system. The law established a Federal Case Registry and National Directory of New Hires to track delinquent parents across state lines. It also required that employers report all new hires to state agencies for transmittal to the national directory and expanded and streamlined procedures for direct withholding of child support from wages. Since the creation of the national directory, more than 3 million parents have been located. This location information is sent to states so child support can be established and enforced.

Streamlined paternity establishment. Paternity establishment is a crucial step toward securing an emotional and financial connection between the father and child. The law streamlined the legal process for paternity establishment, making the process easier and faster. It also expanded the voluntary in-hospital paternity establishment program started in 1993 and required a state affidavit for voluntary paternity acknowledgment. In addition, the law mandated that states publicize the availability and encourage the use of voluntary paternity establishment processes. Individuals who fail to cooperate with paternity establishment will have their monthly TANF assistance reduced.

Tough penalties. Under the law, states can implement tough child support enforcement techniques. The law expanded wage garnishment, allowed states to require participation in work activities in some cases, and authorized states to suspend or revoke driver and professional licenses for parents who owe delinquent child support. The Department of State will deny a passport to an individual who owes more than $5,000 in back child support, resulting in nearly $5 million in child support collections. The President's welfare reform reauthorization proposals would build on this success, reducing the threshold to deny a passport to $2,500 in back child support.

Financial institution data matching. The 1996 welfare reform law included a proposal to match records of delinquent parents with financial institutions. Successful matches are sent to the states within 48 hours so that the states can place a lien on and seize all or part of the accounts identified. In 1998, Congress made it easier for multi-state institutions to match records by using the federal Office of Child Support Enforcement. To date, more than 4,500 financial institutions have agreed to participate.

Access and visitation programs. Since fiscal year 1997, HHS has awarded $10 million each year in block grants to states to promote access and visitation programs to increase non-custodial parents' involvement in their children's lives. The grants may be used to provide such services as mediation, counseling, education, developing of parenting plans, visitation programs, and the development of visitation and custody guidelines.

Promoting marriage and responsible fatherhood. The 1996 welfare reform law recognized that two-parent, married families represent the ideal environment for raising children and therefore featured a variety of family formation provisions. HHS has approved grants and waivers for responsible fatherhood efforts designed to help non-custodial fathers support their children financially and emotionally.

Project Save Our Children. An initiative on criminal child support enforcement, Project Save Our Children is succeeding in its pursuit of chronic delinquent parents who owe large sums of child support. Since the project's creation in 1998, multi-agency regional task forces involving federal and state law enforcement agencies have received and reviewed more than 4,600 referrals, resulting in more than 580 arrests, 450 convictions and civil adjudications, and court orders to pay more than $18 million in owed child support.

New tribal programs. HHS now directly supports tribes, tribal organizations, and Alaskan Native village child support programs for those groups that have applied to establish the programs and have shown that they are able to meet the programs' objectives.

HEALH AND HUMAN SERVICES FATHERHOOD INITIATIVE

Committed parents are crucial to strong and successful families and to the well-being of children. The U.S. Department of Health and Human Services is determined to ensure that its programs and policies recognize the importance of both mothers and fathers and that they support men and women in their roles as parents.

INCREASING FAMILY SELF-SUFFICIENCY

Improving Child Support Collections. An important part of being a responsible parent is providing financial support. Research also suggests that there is a positive relationship between non-custodial fathers' involvement with their children and their payment of child support.

Promoting Employment Opportunities for Low-Income Fathers. Several states are participating in Parents' Fair Share, a demonstration project that provides employment-related training, parenting education, peer group support, and mediation services to encourage low-income fathers to be more involved with their children and increase their payment of child support. In addition, other states have received demonstration grants or waivers through the Office of Child Support Enforcement to allow them to test comprehensive approaches to encourage more responsible fathering by noncustodial parents. Each state project is different, but they all provide a range of needed services,

131

such as job search and training, access and visitation, social services or referral, case management, and child support.

HHS is working closely with the Department of Labor to implement the Welfare to Work program, which provides grants to states and communities to move long-term welfare recipients and certain noncustodial parents of children on welfare into lasting, unsubsidized employment. The Administration's Welfare to Work reauthorization would help more low-income fathers work, pay child support, and play a responsible role in their children's lives. In addition, HHS' Administration for Children and Families (ACF) recently released A Guide to Funding Services for Children and Families through the Temporary Assistance for Needy Families (TANF) Program, which provides examples of ways states could use their TANF funds to support responsible fatherhood efforts and employment of noncustodial parents.

Expanding Partners for Fragile Families. ACF has begun a partnership with the private sector initiative, Partners for Fragile Families. This initiative is aimed at helping fathers work with the mothers of their children in sharing the legal, financial, and emotional responsibilities of parenthood. Activities funded by ACF include Fatherhood Development Workshops on effective practices for working with young unemployed and underemployed fathers, the development of a manual for workers to use in helping low-income fathers learn to interact more effectively with the child support enforcement system, and a peer learning college for child support enforcement experts to identify systemic barriers these young fathers face in becoming responsible fathers. HHS is working with private funders on developing a ten-site Partners for Fragile Families demonstration.

STRENGTHENING PARENT-CHILD BONDS

Encouraging Fathers to "Be Their Dad." In March 1999, HHS launched a new, nationwide public service campaign challenging fathers to remain emotionally and financially connected to their children even if they do not live with them. The campaign's tag line, "They're your kids. Be their dad," stresses the importance of fathers by showing the consequences for children when fathers do not have a positive role in their children's lives. More than a quarter of American children - nearly 17 million - do not live with their father. Girls without fathers in their lives are two and a half times as likely to get pregnant and 53 percent more likely to commit suicide. Boys without fathers in their lives are 63 percent more likely to run away and 37 percent more likely to abuse drugs. Both girls and boys without father involvement are twice as likely to drop out of high school, twice as likely to end up in jail, and nearly four times as likely to need help for emotional or behavioral problems.

Improving Paternity Establishment. ACF has instituted voluntary paternity establishment programs in U.S. hospitals to foster father-child bonds right from the start. Voluntary hospital-based paternity establishment services are required to be available in all hospitals and birthing centers. Some states are reporting that they are establishing paternities in the hospital for over 60 percent of non-marital births.

Promoting Parental Access and Visitation. Since FY 1997, HHS has awarded $10 million in block grant funds annually to all 50 states, the District of Columbia, and U.S. territories to promote access and visitation programs to increase noncustodial parents' involvement in their children's lives. Grant size is based on the number of children in a state not living with both parents. Each state has flexibility in how it designs and operates these programs and can use these funds to provide such services as voluntary or mandatory mediation, counseling, education, development of parenting plans, visitation enforcement (including monitoring, supervision, and neutral drop-off and pick-up), and development of guidelines for visitation and alternative custody arrangements.

Engaging Fathers Early. HHS recognizes that fathers play an important role in their children's early development. The Early Head Start program was specifically designed to ensure maximum involvement of the important men in very young children's lives. A special "Fathers Studies" component has been developed as part of the Early Head Start research and evaluation program to examine the contribution of poor fathers to early childhood development and how program interventions can strengthen father involvement. The Head Start program continues to develop new and innovative ways to increase the parenting skills of both fathers and mothers and to engage them in program activities. Several HHS regional offices have developed partnerships with fraternal organizations to develop programs for encouraging minority fathers in their efforts to be more involved in their children's lives.

PROMOTING HEALTHIER AND SAFER FAMILIES

Improving Infant Health through Father Involvement. The Healthy Start Program was designed to develop strategies at the community level to reduce infant mortality and low-birth weight babies. Several Healthy Start Demonstration Programs have developed male mentoring and fatherhood initiatives as part of their strategy to improve the health of women, children, and families. These initiatives include using male outreach workers to involve fathers, providing job training and links to substance abuse programs for fathers, furnishing transportation and child care services to increase fathers' participation, and developing rites of passage programs for adolescents boys.

Mobilizing for Fathers and Their Special Needs Children. The Health Resources and Services Administration (HRSA) continues to support fathers who have children with developmental disabilities and chronic illness and their families through the National Fathers' Network (NFN). In April 1999, the NFN held a state "Interagency Forum on Fatherhood" in Philadelphia, which brought together male caregivers, public agency and program representatives, family advocacy groups, private organizations, and community-based groups to learn effective strategies in making programs more "father-friendly." The forum also featured the NFN's training video, "Equal Partners, African American Fathers and Systems of Care," which has been distributed to health care providers and programs working with fathers and to the Head Start community. Other activities to support the role of fathers have been funded through HRSA's federal block grants to states. Recent efforts in Washington state, for example, included the State Early Childhood Conference and the annual "Fathers Conference."

Increasing Fathers' Involvement in their Children's Health Care. The Health Care Financing Administration (HCFA) has conducted four focus groups with custodial and non-custodial fathers and mothers to determine barriers to their greater involvement in their children's health care. The focus groups included urban, rural, native Alaskan, and Hispanic-Latino fathers. Information from the focus groups will be used to identify and remove barriers to services.

Reducing Family and Community Violence. As part of the Administration's comprehensive strategy to prevent domestic violence, HHS convened a meeting with fatherhood programs to discuss the issues of domestic violence within the context of Temporary Assistance for Needy Families (TANF) requirements to cooperate in the establishment of paternity and child support. State demonstrations have been funded to examine issues of domestic violence and custodial parents' non-cooperation with the child support enforcement requirements. HHS coordinated a multi-year cooperative agreement with a consortium of Historically Black Colleges and Universities to develop models to prevent minority male violence. Finally, the Centers for Disease Control and Prevention (CDC) is working to reduce family and community violence, particularly among young boys and adolescent males.

Connecting Fathers to Communities through Public-Private Partnerships. HHS and its regional offices have sponsored a variety of forums to bring together local public and private organizations and individuals to support fathers' involvement in their families and communities. For example, Region V convened a Fatherhood Initiative Forum in Detroit, Mich., and a Title X Family Planning Conference in Chicago, Ill., to discuss strategies for promoting male involvement in teen pregnancy prevention. In addition, regions VIII, IX, and X joined other organizations in supporting a "Strengthening Families through Public/Private Partnerships: Connecting Fathers" Conference in Oakland, Calif. Finally, ACF joined fatherhood and foundation partners in convening a "Listening Session on Tribal Fatherhood Issues" to identify the needs of fathers and families in tribal communities.

PREVENTING PREMATURE FATHERHOOD

Increasing Reproductive Health Outreach to Young Men. Through HHS regional offices, small grants have been awarded to Title X family planning clinics to develop pilot programs designed to prevent premature fatherhood. These projects employ male high school students as interns to provide them with on-the-job training in clinic operations and allied health occupations and education about male responsibility, family planning and reproductive health.

Promoting Family Planning Services for Men. Twenty community-based organizations specializing in educational and social services for men have been awarded almost $3 million in grants to develop and implement family planning and reproductive health services. A specialized training plan for project staff was established in FY 1999 to integrate research findings on male reproductive health activities into male-oriented programs.

Information on Prevention Programs for Boys and Young Men. Projects have also been funded to identify abstinence programs for boys and young men and to develop a strategy to provide information to states and local communities on promising abstinence and contraceptive-based programs.

WHICH INITIATIVES CAN BE HELPFUL TO ME?

NOTES

CASE INFORMATION

CHILD SUPPORT ENFORCEMENT RECORDS

Custodial Parent_____

Address _____

_____

Names of Dependent Children/ Dates of Birth

_____ _____

_____ _____

_____ _____

_____ _____

Noncustodial Parent_____

Address(es) _____

_____

_____

Social Security Number/ Date and Place of Birth

_____ _____

Employer(s)/ Dates

_____ _____
_____ _____
_____ _____
_____ _____

Child Support Enforcement Office

_____

_____

_____

Enforcement caseworker

_____

_____

Case Number _____

State Enforcement Agency

_____

_____

_____

Lawyer _____

_____

Courts:
Custodial Parent _____

_____

Noncustodial Parent _____

Present Support Obligation: $_____

To be paid _____

NOTES

CHILD SUPPORT ENFORCEMENT CASE LOG

Action Taken_____

_____

_____

_____

_____

_____

_____

_____

_____

Date _____

Outcome_____

_____

_____

_____

Action Taken_____

_____

_____

_____

_____

_____

_____

_____

_____

Date _____

Outcome_____

_____

_____

_____

Action Taken_____

_____

_____

_____

_____

_____

_____

_____

_____

Date _____

Outcome_____

_____

_____

_____

Action Taken _____

_____

_____

_____

_____

_____

_____

_____

_____

Date _____

Outcome _____

_____

_____

_____

Action Taken_____

_____

_____

_____

_____

_____

_____

_____

Date _____

Outcome_____

_____

_____

_____

ction Taken_____

_____

_____

_____

_____

_____

_____

_____

_____

)ate _____

)utcome_____

_____

_____

_____

Action Taken_____

_____

_____

_____

_____

_____

_____

_____

_____

_____

Date _____

Outcome_____

_____

_____

_____

NOTES

NOTES

SAMPLE CHILD SUPPORT ENFORCEMENT APPLICATION

SAMPLE CUSTODIAL PARENT APPLICATION

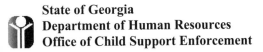

State of Georgia
Department of Human Resources
Office of Child Support Enforcement

Instructions for Custodial Parent / Custodian
Application for Child Support Services

You must complete a separate Application for **each** parent from whom you are seeking support. If you **are not** the mother of the children, an Application for Child Support Services must be completed on **both** the mother and father of the children.

Custodial Parent or Custodian (CP/CU) is the person who lives with the children.
Non-Custodial Parent "(NCP)" is the person who is responsible for paying child support.

Be sure you use these titles correctly, or the Office of Child Support Enforcement may attempt to collect money from the person who is already living with, and caring for the children.

You must answer **all** questions in this application packet. If a question does not apply, please write "N/A" (i.e., non-applicable). If you do not know the answer to a question, write "UNK" (i.e., unknown).

EVERYONE who applies for child support services **must** provide copies of the following:
- Your driver's license or other picture ID;
- Proof of YOUR income;
- Social Security Cards and Birth Certificates for all claimed children;
- All court orders or divorce decrees that involve these children. Certified copies are preferred.

Note: Failure to provide copies of all existing orders could result in unnecessary delays and/or loss of personal/legal jurisdiction.

Applicants who **do not** receive Temporary Assistance For Needy Families (TANF) or Medical Assistance must pay an application fee of $25 for services. **This fee must be paid in the form of a money order. This fee is non-refundable.** If you are applying for services from more than one non-custodial parent at this time, only one application fee will be charged.

Your application **must** meet these requirements:
- All questions are answered completely, to the best of your knowledge
- You have provided the items requested above
- Your signature is notarized at all the required places

If you require assistance in completing this form, you may request an appointment with an agency representative. Otherwise, your application will be reviewed and assigned to a Locate Technician.

Custodial Parent / Custodian
Statements of Understanding

I _____, SSN_____ hereby contract with the Office of Child Support Enforcement (OCSE) to provide appropriate child support services. This application constitutes the contract and its terms. I understand that OCSE determines which services are necessary for me. If any application fee is required, no services will begin until the fee is paid.

I understand that: (please initial each statement)

_____ The $25 application fee is **non-refundable** and is required to process my new application. If I currently receive Temporary Assistance For Needy Families (TANF) or Medicaid (MAO), this fee is **waived**. Federal regulations 45 CFR §302.33 authorize the Office of Child Support Enforcement to charge an application fee and to recover the costs of any services performed for applicants who **are not** receiving public assistance (TANF).

_____ Georgia Law, O.C.G.A. §19-11-6(c) provides that an application for services by persons not receiving TANF is an assignment to OCSE of their right to receive child support;

_____ I am authorizing the Office of Child Support Enforcement to:
- Locate the non-custodial parent;
- Establish the legal paternity of my child(ren);
- Obtain a legal order for child support including medical insurance for the child(ren), if available at reasonable cost in accordance with O.C.G.A. §19-6-15;
- To review and modify my child support order, upon written request, every three years or at an earlier date if there is a significant change in circumstances in accordance with Georgia Law, O.C.G.A. §19-11-12;
- Enforce the child support order as permitted by law;
- Collect and distribute child support payments through the OCSE Family Support Registry.

_____ The child support agent or assigned representative who is handling my case will contact the non-custodial parent of my child(ren) and set up a meeting with him/her to get them to agree to pay child support. The amount of child support to be paid generally will be based on his/her income. If I have any information that I believe the child support enforcement office should know about for this meeting (such as the non-custodial parent's income), I must contact their office immediately. Otherwise, an agreement may be reached on the amount of child support to be paid based on other information, including what the non-custodial parent tells the agent.

_____ I must agree to submit myself and/or the child(ren) in this case to genetic testing, if necessary, for OCSE to provide the requested services.

_____ OCSE may use an attorney to establish or enforce my child support order. The attorney represents the interests of OCSE and no attorney-client relationship exists between the attorney and me. The attorney cannot handle any other legal matter such as custody or visitation. [Georgia Law, O.C.G.A. §19-11-23 (b) and §19-11-53].

_____ I must notify OCSE of any changes to my name, address, phone number or any other information that is needed to properly manage my case and assure prompt mailing of payments due me. Any new information about the non-custodial parent will be provided to assist in the location and enforcement of my case against the non-custodial parent.

_____ If I do not cooperate with the OCSE and my case is closed, I agree to repay any expenses incurred on my behalf. This includes costs of services such as court costs that the child support enforcement office is liable for as a result of a court action being dismissed if I close my case. OCSE may also close my case for a minimum of six (6) months based on non-cooperation.

_____ Whenever possible, I should submit my questions or requests for information about my case, in writing. This may prevent any misunderstanding of verbal messages and will assist OCSE in investigating and preparing answers to my inquiries.

_____ If I have a valid complaint about the way my case is being handled, I have a right to request a formal review by OCSE management.

I further understand that: (please initial each statement)

____ Disclosure of my circumstances in pleadings or other documents may be filed in a proceeding to enforce and/or to determine child support for my child(ren). If I believe that disclosure of my information would endanger my family's health, safety or liberty, I may request a hearing under Georgia Law, O.C.G.A. §19-11-30 and O.C.G.A. §19-11-131 and may receive a finding of nondisclosure of information. [Refer to page 7 of the Application].

____ To assure the privacy of my case information, information will only be discussed with me. No discussions can be made with my spouse, friends or relatives on my behalf.

____ Federal law requires OCSE to intercept state and federal tax refunds to repay past due child support when the non-custodial parent owes past-due support. OCSE will notify the Internal Revenue Service (IRS) and the Georgia Department of Revenue to withhold up to the total past due amount from the Non-Custodial Parent's tax refunds. [45 CFR §303.72 & O.C.G.A. §48-7-160].

____ If my order was issued in Georgia, OCSE is authorized to calculate and collect interest on overdue child support pursuant to Georgia Law, O.C.G.A. §7-4-12.1. Any court or administrative order issued outside the state of Georgia may or may not be subject to interest. Interest will only be collected on out of state child support orders when the referring agency calculates the interest and/or there is an order adjudicating the interest in terms of a specific dollar amount.

____ Any state and federal refunds collected by OCSE will first be applied toward any past debt owed to the State by the non-custodial parent, before I receive any portion of the refund.

____ If a Federal tax refund is intercepted from a joint return the IRS must determine what portion, if any, is due my case. The IRS may adjust the amount of a refund based on the joint filing and can do so for up to six years. I will be responsible for repaying OCSE for any monies that I received incorrectly. If a State tax refund is intercepted from a joint return, OCSE will determine what portion, if any, is due my case.

Federal/State tax monies could possibly take up to six months to be distributed to me due to State and Federal laws, administrative hearings or joint refund issues.

____ All child support is received and posted at the Georgia Family Support Registry. Based on Federal Regulations, all payments are pro-rated by the non-custodial parent's social security number to all cases.

____ I must notify OCSE if I apply for and receive TANF (cash) benefits. If I do not, I may receive overpayments in child support that I am not entitled to and I may have to repay the State.

____ If I receive any child support payment in error, OCSE will notify me of the mistake **in writing**. I understand that I may either repay this entire amount within the time allotted in my notice, or I can have the amount taken out in installments from any future child support payments. Unless I object to this action, installment deductions will be made at a minimum of 10% of each payment or $10, whichever is greater, until the erroneous payment is paid in full. Do you agree? [ ] Yes [ ] No

If I object in person or by phone, I have the right to an explanation. If I disagree with the explanation provided, OCSE will request an administrative hearing on my behalf with the Office of State Administrative Hearings.

I have received and read all program information describing available services, fees, rights and responsibilities, collection policies and distribution procedures. I am submitting all completed information with this application. I certify that all of the information supplied by me is true and correct to the best of my knowledge and belief. My signature on this document constitutes a contract and authorizes the Office of Child Support Enforcement to provide necessary and appropriate services on my behalf.

Under the penalty of perjury I do hereby swear and affirm that the information I provided on the Application for Child Support Services is accurate and true to the best of my knowledge. I understand the criminal penalties for making false statements and false swearing under O.C.G.A. §16-10-71 is punishable by a fine of not more than $1,000 or by imprisonment of one year or more, or both. I do hereby attest to the truthfulness of the information provided.

_____   _____

Applicant Signature   Date

TANF HISTORY OF APPLICANT (if applicable)   If you never received TANF, skip to next section

[ ] I currently receive TANF benefits [ ] I currently receive Medicaid Only [ ] I currently receive Food Stamps only
[ ] Formerly on TANF; TANF received from _____ to _____

IV-D Application and Assignment for Child Support Services
Custodial Parent / Custodian Case Information

Please complete the following information about yourself, the absent non-custodial parent and child(ren) for whom you wish to receive our services. The more information you can tell us, the better we will be able to serve you.

You must notify us immediately if you have a change of address. We can only update you on our progress or send support to you if we have your current mailing address.

TYPE OF SERVICE REQUESTED

[ ] Locate of NCP Only   [ ] Establishment /
Enforcement of court order **(full service cases only)**
[ ] Collection and Distribution – No enforcement
actions will be taken
[ ] Medical Insurance Only – Generally applies to Former
TANF and Medicaid Only applicants
[ ] **Full Services (all of the above services)**

CUSTODIAL PARENT/ CUSTODIAN IDENTIFYING INFORMATION

Your Name: _____

Last   First   Middle   Maiden

Social Security Number: _____ | Date of Birth: _____

Sex: [ ] Male [ ] Female | Home Pho

Marital Status: [ ] Single   [ ] Married | If married, current spouse: _____
[ ] Separated [ ] Divorced on _____ | Date of Marriage: _____

Home Address: _____

Street Address   City   County   State   Zip

Mailing Address: _____

P.O. Box   City   County   State   Zip

May we contact you at work? [ ] Yes [ ] No | Work Pho

E-Mail Address: _____ | Cellular P

Your relationship to the child(ren) | [ ] Biological Parent [ ] Custodian [ ] Legal Guardian
| [ ] Relative [ ] Other: _____

Note: If you are not the biological parent of the child(ren), you must complete an application for services for both biological parents, if living. Please complete appropriate section on page 4.

NON-CUSTODIAL PARENT FROM WHOM YOU NEED SUPPORT

| Last | First | Middle | Social Security Number | [ ] Male [ ] Female | Birth Date | Race |

If NCP is married, does he have any Natural or Adopted children by his current spouse? If so, list on page 6.

CHILD #1 OF THE NCP FOR WHOM YOU ARE SEEKING SUPPORT

| Last | First | Middle | Social Security Number | [ ] Male [ ] Female | Race |
| Birth date: | Place of Birth: | | CITY | STATE | |

CHILD #2 OF THE NCP FOR WHOM YOU ARE SEEKING SUPPORT

| Last | First | Middle | Social Security Number | [ ] Male [ ] Female | Race |
| Birth date: | Place of Birth: | | CITY | STATE | |

application_cp.doc   3   Revised December 24, 2002

CHILD #3 OF THE NCP FOR WHOM YOU ARE SEEKING SUPPORT

Last	First	Middle	Social Security Number	[ ] Male [ ] Female	Race
Birth date:	Place of Birth:				
			CITY	STATE	

CUSTODIAL PARENT / CUSTODIAN EMPLOYMENT AND INCOME INFORMATION

Employer:

Address:

Street Address	City	County	State	Zip

GROSS MONTHLY INCOME SOURCES

Salary/Wages/Self employment Income:	$	Disability benefits	$
Bonuses, commissions, allowances, overtime, tips, etc	$	Worker's Compensation Benefits	$
Child Support	$	Alimony / Spousal Support	$
Social Security benefits (SSI, RSDI)	$	Unemployment compensation	$
Pension, retirement, or annuity payments	$	Interest, dividends and 1099 income	$
Income from royalties, trusts, or estates	$	Rental income	$
Reimbursed expenses or in-kind payments to the extent that they reduce expenses			$
Capital gains on sale or exchange of property unless non-recurring income imputed from above assets			$
Other:	$	**Total Monthly Income**	$

HEALTH INSURANCE INFORMATION (if children on this case are or can be insured by applicant)

Insurance Co. Name:	Phone No.:
Address:	

CUSTODIAL PARENT / CUSTODIAN MONTHLY EXPENSES

Rent or Mortgage	$	Utilities (Electric, Gas, Phone)	$		
Medical Insurance Premiums	$	Child Care	$	Other	$
Medical Bills or Expenses	$				

CUSTODIAL PARENT / CUSTODIAN FAMILY HISTORY

Mother:	Phone No.:
Date of Birth:	Deceased on:
Address:	

Street Address	City	County	State	Zip

Father:	Phone No.:
Date of Birth:	Deceased on:
Address:	

Street Address	City	County	State	Zip

Complete this section only if you are not the child(ren)'s Biological Parent

I _____ am the custodian or the following child(ren).

_____   _____

_____   _____

My relationship to the child(ren) is _____ .
The child(ren) came to live with me on _____ .

Biological Mother: If Deceased, please note.

Name	Address	City	County	State	State	Zip	Date of Birth	SSN

application_cp.doc   4   Revised December 24, 2002

163

Biological Father: If Deceased, please note.									
Name	Address	City	County	State	State	Zip	Date of Birth	SSN	

Custodian's Signature   **Date**

Non-Custodial Parent Information This is the person who DOES NOT live with the child(ren).

NCP NAME				
	Last	First	Middle	Jr / Sr / Maiden

Alias, nicknames, etc.:

Marital Status: [ ] Single   [ ] Married   [ ] Divorced

Social Security Number:

Place of Birth:

	City	State	County	Country

Eyes: | Hair:

Mailing Address: Does the NCP Own This or Other Property? [ ] Yes [ ] No

	Street Address	City	County	State	Zip

Is home address [ ] Current or [ ] Last known   Phone Number: Cellular/Other Phone:

Other Possible Address:

	Street Address	City	County	State	Zip

Driver's License No: State:

Vehicle Make/Model/Year:

Name of Bank:

NCP's BANKRUPTCY HISTORY

Do you know if the NCP has filed Bankruptcy? If so, when?_____

NCP MILITARY STATUS

[ ] Never in Military
Service; [ ] Active; [ ]
Retired; [ ] Discharged.
Branch:_____

_____ Service
No:_____

____
Entry
Date:_____
_____Discharge
Date:_____

NCP PRISON / CORRECTIONAL INSTITUTION HISTORY

[ ] Never incarcerated [ ] Incarcerated in Past [ ] Currently incarcerated

Incarcerated from _____ to _____   Due to be Released: _____

Institution Name:

Institution Address:

Parole Officer: | Phone No.:

NCP'S FAMILY HISTORY   [This is helpful even if NCP's parents are deceased].

NCP's Mother: | Phone No.:

Date of Birth: | Place of Birth: | Deceased on:

Address:

	Street Address	City	County	State	Zip

NCP's Father: | Phone No.:

Date of Birth: | Place of Birth: | Deceased on:

Address:

	Street Address	City		County	State	Zip
Other known Relative:			Relationship to NCP:			
Address:						
	Street Address	City		County	State	Zip
Phone Number or other contact address (friends, etc)						
	Street Address	City		County	State	Zip

NCP EMPLOYMENT AND INCOME SOURCES

[ ] Unemployed [ ] Self-employed	Type of Business:

Employer:	Job title:
Contact Person:	Phone No.:

Address:

	Street Address	City	County	State	Zip	
Employed from:		to				[ ] Union:
How Often Paid? [ ] Weekly [ ] Bi-weekly [ ] Monthly [ ] Semi-monthly						
Gross income: $		per				Attach Pay stubs, if possib

Does NCP have a 401k or other Pension Plan with this employer? [ ] Yes   Specify:_____

OTHER WORK / RETIREMENT / PENSION PLAN INCOME

Has NCP ever worked for a Federal Government Agency? If so, what agency:

Does NCP receive Federal Benefits? [ ] Social Security   [ ] Postal   [ ]RR Retirement   [ ]Civil Service
                                    [ ] Military [ ]
VA [ ]Retirement

Does NCP receive Unemployment Benefits? [ ] Yes [ ] No

Does NCP have Pension Plan benefits? [ ] Yes   If so, from where?_____

List all sources of income in monthly gross amounts:	**Source**	**Amount**
		$_____
	_____	$_____

NCP HEALTH INSURANCE INFORMATION

Health & Sickness insurance [ ] IS [ ] IS NOT available through the NCP's employer

Who is currently covered by Insurance?

Insurance Co. Name:	Phone No.:

Address:

	Street Address	City	County	State	Zip
Policy/Group No.:					
Cost per paycheck for individual coverage: $		for family coverage: $			

PROFESSIONAL LICENSES HELD BY NCP

List any known or suspected licenses_____

NCP's OTHER ASSETS / PROPERTY / INVESTMENTS   [if available]

Asset Description	Value
	$
	$

NATURAL OR ADOPTED CHILDREN FOR WHOM THE NCP IS LEGALLY RESPONSIBLE TO SUPPORT (Please do not list step children)			
Name of Child	Date of Birth	Name of Other Parent	Name of Person the child lives with

COURT ORDERS, SUPPORT ORDERS, AND ARREARAGE OWED

Note: Check each type of order. You MUST provide a copy of the order(s) to be enforced

[ ] **There is NO Court Order** requiring either parent to pay support for the children of this case, because:	
[ ] I am currently married to the NCP (no divorce)	Marriage Da

[ ] I was never married to the NCP. (You MUST complete a Paternity Affidavit for each child of this NCP)

[ ] **DIVORCE DECREE   [ ] OCSE SUPPORT ORDER   [ ] LEGITIMATION ORDER**
Filed in   County, State of   on   [ ]NCP not ordered to pay child support.
Support Ordered Amount: $ per   [ ] For each child [ ] For All children
There is an Arrearage (overdue) of $ as of   Complete the attached Arrearage Affidavit*

[ ] **CONTEMPT ORDER   [ ] MODIFICATION ORDER**
Filed in   County, State of   on   [ ]NCP not ordered to pay child support.
Support Ordered Amount: $ per   [ ] For each child [ ] For All children
There is an Arrearage (overdue) of $ as of   Complete the attached Arrearage Affidavit*

[ ] **URESA / UIFSA ORDER   (support order from another state)   Note: We must have "certified" copies**
Filed in   County, State of   on   [ ]NCP not ordered to pay child support.
Support Ordered Amount: $ per   [ ] For each child [ ] For All children
There is an Arrearage (overdue) of $ as of   Complete the attached Arrearage Affidavit*

*Note: If there is more than one court order, an Affidavit of Arrears may need to be completed for each order.

Complete this section <u>only</u> if there is a history of domestic violence

Have criminal charges ever filed been filed against the NCP?
[ ] **Yes** [ ] **No**

Has the Non-Custodial Parent ever caused you or your child(ren) any physical or emotional harm?
[ ] **Yes** [ ] **No**

If you said **Yes**, please provide any documentation you have to support this allegation such as a Restraining Order, Protective Order, relevant Court or Police Reports or other written statements, if available.

Under Georgia Law, O.C.G.A. §19-11-30 and §19-11-130, OCSE will not release any information that would place you or your children at risk of physical or emotional harm. In such instances, a Family Violence Indicator will be activated on your child support case.

PRIVATE CHILD SUPPORT CASE HISTORY If this does not apply, skip to next section	
Do you have an active child support case with any other state agency, private attorney or a private collection agency for the child(ren) listed on this application?	[__]Yes If so, list below: Where:_____ When: _____

CHILD SUPPORT PAYMENT AND ARREARAGE RECORD

Please show the total amount of support **owed and received** each month. Receipts, canceled checks, payment records, etc. may be requested to prove the information in this affidavit.

Year	Amount		Year	Amount		Year	Amount	
	Due	Paid		Due	Paid		Due	Paid
Jan	$	$	Jan	$	$	Jan	$	$
Feb	$	$	Feb	$	$	Feb	$	$
Mar	$	$	Mar	$	$	Mar	$	$
Apr	$	$	Apr	$	$	Apr	$	$
May	$	$	May	$	$	May	$	$
Jun	$	$	Jun	$	$	Jun	$	$
Jul	$	$	Jul	$	$	Jul	$	$
Aug	$	$	Aug	$	$	Aug	$	$
Sep	$	$	Sep	$	$	Sep	$	$
Oct	$	$	Oct	$	$	Oct	$	$
Nov	$	$	Nov	$	$	Nov	$	$
Dec	$	$	Dec	$	$	Dec	$	$
YTD Total	$	$	YTD Total	$	$	YTD Total	$	$

Year	Amount		Year	Amount		Year	Amount	
	Due	Paid		Due	Paid		Due	Paid
Jan	$	$	Jan	$	$	Jan	$	$
Feb	$	$	Feb	$	$	Feb	$	$
Mar	$	$	Mar	$	$	Mar	$	$
Apr	$	$	Apr	$	$	Apr	$	$
May	$	$	May	$	$	May	$	$
Jun	$	$	Jun	$	$	Jun	$	$
Jul	$	$	Jul	$	$	Jul	$	$
Aug	$	$	Aug	$	$	Aug	$	$
Sep	$	$	Sep	$	$	Sep	$	$
Oct	$	$	Oct	$	$	Oct	$	$
Nov	$	$	Nov	$	$	Nov	$	$
Dec	$	$	Dec	$	$	Dec	$	$
YTD Total	$	$	YTD Total	$	$	YTD Total	$	$

Total Due:$_____ Minus Total Paid:$_____ = Balance Due: $_____ as of _____.

I certify that all of the information supplied by me is true and correct to the best of my knowledge and belief. I understand the criminal penalties for making false statements and false swearing under O.C.G.A. §16-10-71 and do hereby attest to the truthfulness of the information provided.

My Signature:_____ Date: _____

Copies may be made if additional pages are needed

Paternity Affidavit

This form is REQUIRED for each child on this case if one of the following situations applies:

- Parents were not married at the time the child was conceived or born;
- There is no Court document establishing LEGAL paternity for the child listed; or
- If paternity is in doubt for some other reason.

Child's Birth Certificate Name			
	Last	First	Middle

[ ] Male [ ] Female

Sex

Child was conceived in:
        City   State

Hospital where child was born:
        City   State

Mother's Marital Status at child's birth:

Were the Mother and Alleged Father ever married to each other? [ ] Yes [ ] No
If so, When?   Where (City, State)?

If mother was married to another man at birth, to whom?

Date parents began sexual relationship:

Did Mother have intercourse with anyone else within 45 days of becoming pregnant?   [ ] Yes [ ] No [ ] Unsure
If so, who?

       Name   Address   City   County   State   Zip

Has Mother ever named anyone else as the father of this child?   [ ] Yes [ ] No [ ] Unsure

If so, name:

Who is the alleged father?

Did the alleged father (NCP) ever sign a paternity statement or acknowledge paternity of this child? When? Where?

Has NCP provided child support, necessities, or gifts for this child? In what way?

Has paternity testing ever been done regarding this NCP? What were the results? (Attach copy of results)

Has paternity testing ever been done on any other man? If yes, who and what were the results? (Attach copy of results)

Personally appeared before the undersigned officer, duly authorized to administer oaths, the undersigned who states under oath that the foregoing statements regarding paternity are true and correct. I understand that medical tests may be required to establish legal paternity for the above child(ren). I am willing to cooperate with OCSE regarding genetic testing and legal actions to establish paternity for the child(ren).

I certify that all of the information supplied by me is true and correct to the best of my knowledge and belief. I understand the criminal penalties for making false statements and false swearing under O.C.G.A. §16-10-71 and do hereby attest to the truthfulness of the information provided.

Your Signature: _____ Date: _____

Notary Public Signature: _____ Commission Expiration Date: _____

NOTARY SEAL

Copies may be made if additional pages are needed

INFORMATION I MUST GATHER FOR MY APPLICATION

SAMPLE NONCUSTODIAL PARENT APPLICATION

State of Georgia
Department of Human Resources
Office of Child Support Enforcement

Instructions for Non-Custodial Applicant Application for Child Support Services

Custodial Parent or Custodian (CP/CU) is the person who lives with the children.
Non-Custodial Parent / Applicant "(NCP)" is the person who is attempting to establis
paternity and/or responsible for paying child support.

Be sure you use these titles correctly, or the Office of Child Support Enforcement may attemp
to collect money from the person who is already living with and caring for the children.

You must answer **all** questions in this application packet. If a question does not apply, pleas
write "N/A" (i.e., non-applicable). If you do not know the answer to a question, write "UNK" (i.e
unknown).

EVERYONE who applies for child support services **must** provide copies of the following:
* Your driver's license or other picture ID;
* Proof of YOUR income (2 current pay stubs, W-2, last 2 years tax returns);
* Your Social Security Card
* All court orders or divorce decree that involve these children. Certified copies are preferred.

Note: Failure to provide copies of all existing orders could result in unnecessary delays and/c
loss of personal/legal jurisdiction.

Applicants must pay an application fee of $25 for services if the CP/CU is not presently a TAN
or Medicaid recipient in Georgia or any other state. **This fee must be paid in the form of
money order. This fee is non-refundable**.

Your application **must** meet these requirements:
* All questions are answered completely, to the best of your knowledge
* You have provided the items requested above
* Your signature is notarized at all the required places

If you require assistance in completing this form, you may request an appointment with a
agency representative. Otherwise, your application will be reviewed and assigned to a Loca
Technician.

Note: You must complete a separate Application for **each** parent for whom you are seeking t
establish paternity and/or provide child support.

Non-Custodial Applicant Statements of Understanding

_____, SSN_____ hereby contract with the Georgia Office of Child Support Enforcement (OCSE) to provide appropriate child support services. This application constitutes the contract and its terms. I understand that OCSE determines which services are necessary for me. If any application fee is required, no services will begin until the fee is paid.

I understand that: (please initial each statement)

__ The $25 application fee is **non-refundable** and is required to process my new application unless the CP/CU is currently on Temporary Assistance For Needy Families (TANF) or Medicaid (MAO). If so, we will take whatever actions are necessary and this fee will be **waived**. Federal regulations 45 CFR §302.33 authorize the Office of Child Support Enforcement to charge an application fee and to recover the costs of any services performed for applicants.

__ I **must** provide a valid address for the custodial parent (CP). OCSE will not process this application without a complete address on the Custodial Parent. OCSE is **prohibited** by federal regulations from attempting to locate the CP or my children, except in connection with the Parental Kidnapping Prevention Act.

__ By applying for services, I am authorizing OCSE to provide all applicable services:
♣establishing the legal paternity of my child(ren),
♣establishing a legal order for child support including medical insurance for the child(ren), if available to me at reasonable cost in accordance with O.C.G.A. §19-6-15, or enforcing an existing child support order.

All child support orders:
* Are subject to immediate income deduction [support deducted from my paycheck];
* Are subject to future review and modification [upward or downward depending upon my financial circumstances]; and
* Will be enforced by legal action taken against me if I fail to comply with the support order as permitted by law;
* Are subject to review and modification, upon written request, every three years or at an earlier date if there is a significant change in circumstances in accordance with O.C.G.A. § 19-11-12;
* OCSE is authorized to calculate and collect interest on overdue child support orders issued in Georgia pursuant to O.C.G.A. §7-4-12.1. Interest on out of state orders is subject to the laws of the issuing state or country;
* Are subject to collection and distribution through OCSE Family Support Registry.

__ The child support agent or assigned representative who is handling my case will contact the custodial parent or custodian of my child(ren) and set up a meeting with them. I understand that the CP/CU may assert that their and/or the child(ren)'s health, safety or liberty would be put at unreasonable risk if OCSE acted on my application for services. Therefore, unless the CP/CU has an active TANF or Medicaid case, OCSE cannot compel them to cooperate in proceedings to determine child support for my child(ren) and/or enforce a support order. If such an assertion is made or if the CP/CU's cooperation is required but cannot be obtained, OCSE will close my case and cease further actions on my behalf. The $25 application fee **will not** be refunded.

__ I must agree to submit to genetic testing if necessary to establish paternity. Upon receipt of positive results, I will cooperate by signing a consent order to pay support based on the Georgia Guidelines, O.C.G.A. §19-6-15 and, under certain conditions, reimburse the state for any genetic testing fees;

__ If I have a **valid** complaint about the way my case is being handled, I have a right to request a formal review by OCSE management;

__ I must not make any further direct payments to the CP/CU once a support obligation is put in place by OCSE and I understand that I may not receive credit for such payments;

I further understand that: (please initial each statement)

____ OCSE may use an attorney to establish or enforce my child support order. The attorney represents the interests of OCSE and no attorney-client relationship exists between the attorney and me. Georgia Law, O.C.G.A. §19-11-23 (b) and §19-11-53]. The attorney cannot handle any other legal matter such as custody or visitation.

____ If the Office of Child Support Enforcement accepts my case, I agree to repay any expenses incurred on my behalf. This includes costs of services such as court costs that the child support office is liable for as a result of a court action being dismissed;

____ I must notify OCSE of any changes to my name, address, phone number or any other information that is needed to properly manage my case to ensure prompt enforcement of payments due from me.

____ To assure the privacy of my case information, information will only be discussed with me. No discussions can be made with my spouse, friends or relatives on my behalf.

____ Federal law requires OCSE to intercept state and federal tax refunds to repay past due child support when a non-custodial parent owes past-due support. OCSE will notify the Internal Revenue Service (IRS) and the Georgia Department of Revenue to withhold up to the total past due amount from my tax refunds. [45 CFR §303.72 & O.C.G.A. §48-7-160].

____ Any state and federal refunds collected by OCSE will first be applied toward any past debt owed to the State and then applied to any debt owed to the CP/CU by me, before I receive any portion of the refund.

____ If a Federal tax refund is intercepted from a joint return, the IRS must determine what portion, if any, is due my case. The IRS may adjust the amount of a refund based on the joint filing and can do so for up to six years.

If a State tax refund is intercepted from a joint return, OCSE will determine what portion, if any, is due my spouse if I should ask for a review.

Federal/State tax monies could possibly take up to six months to be distributed to my child(ren) due to State and Federal laws, administrative hearings or joint refund issues.

____ All child support is received and posted at the Georgia Family Support Registry. Based on Federal Regulations, all payments are pro-rated by my social security number to all of my cases payable through the Georgia Family Support Registry.

____ If I receive monies from OCSE in error, OCSE will notify me of the mistake and will provide an explanation in person or by phone. The monies will be recouped from future child support payments until paid in full.

I have received and read all program information describing available services, fees, rights and responsibilities, collection policies and distribution procedures. I am submitting all completed information with this application. I certify that all of the information supplied by me is true and correct to the best of my knowledge and belief. My signature on this document constitutes a contract and authorizes the Office of Child Support Enforcement to provide necessary and appropriate services on my behalf.

Under the penalty of perjury I do hereby swear and affirm that the information I provided on the Application for Child Support Services is accurate and true to the best of my knowledge. understand the criminal penalties for making false statements and false swearing under O.C.G.A. §16-10-71 is punishable by a fine of not more than $1,000 or by imprisonment of one year or more, or both. I do hereby attest to the truthfulness of the information provided.

_____   _____
Signature   Date

SUPPLEMENTAL QUESTIONS FOR NON-CUSTODIAL APPLICANT

1. Please state the full name, gender, date of birth and race for each child of the Custodial Parent for whom you claim to be the father:

NAME	GENDER	DATE OF BIRTH	RACE
_____	[ ] M [ ] F	___/___/___	_____
_____	[ ] M [ ] F	___/___/___	_____
_____	[ ] M [ ] F	___/___/___	_____
_____	[ ] M [ ] F	___/___/___	_____
_____	[ ] M [ ] F	___/___/___	_____

2. Please state the name and, if known to you, the address of any **other** man claiming to be the father of any of the children named in response to question #1 above: _____

3. Please state the name and, if known to you, the address of any **other** man who, to the best of your knowledge, was or may have been married to the mother of any of the children named in response to question #1 above at the time of the birth or the probable time of conception of such children: _____

4. Please state the name and, if known to you, the address of any other man who, to the best of your knowledge was or may have been adjudicated by a court or administrative agency to be the father of any of the children named in response to question #1 above: _____

5. Please state the name and, if known to you, the address of any other man who, to the best of your knowledge was or may have been at any time the adoptive father of any of the children named in response to question #1 above: _____

6. Please state the name and if known to you, the address of any other man, who to the best of your knowledge may presently be residing with the Custodial Parent and/or any of the children named in response to question #1 above. Please state, if known to you, the relationship of such man to the Custodial Parent (boyfriend, husband, etc): _____

7. Please describe your relationship with the Custodial Parent at the present time:
   a. Are you in regular contact with the Custodial Parent?   [ ] Yes [ ] No
   b. Is your relationship generally cordial?   [ ] Yes [ ] No
   c. Have you discussed with the Custodial Parent your desire to have a support order entered by an appropriate court?   [ ] Yes [ ] N/A
   d. Do you feel the Custodial Parent would cooperate with OCSE?   [ ] Yes [ ] No
   e. Does the child(ren) know that you are/may be their father?   [ ] Yes [ ] No
   f. Do you have a good relationship with the child(ren)?   [ ] Yes [ ] No

8. Do you understand that once begun, an action for a support order may not be terminated merely upon your request?   [ ] Yes [ ] No

9. Do you understand that, once begun, administrative and/or legal proceedings for a support order may require you to provide documentation and information concerning your financial circumstances, employment history and family obligations?   [ ] Yes [ ] No

10. Do you understand that **no other issues** such as custody or visitation can or will be addressed in any support order obtained incident to this action. That if you **do** wish to address such issues, you must do so on your own, in separate legal proceedings?   [ ] Yes [ ] No

11. Do you understand that even if a child support order already exists, that if the CP says that they feel they or the child(ren) might be at risk of physical or emotional harm if OCSE registers a case, we will NOT be able to proceed on your application?   [ ] Yes [ ] No

My answers to these supplemental questions are true and accurate to the best of my knowledge.

_____   _____
Signature   Date

IV-D Application and Assignment for Child Support Services
Non-Custodial Applicant Case Information

Please complete the following information about yourself, the non-custodial applicant and the child(ren) for whom you wish to receive our services. The more information you can tell us, the better we will be able to serve you. If you need assistance in completing this information, please contact your local child support enforcement office. **Please notify us immediately if you have a change of address. We can only assist you with this case if we have a current mailing address.**

SERVICES PROVIDED ARE "ALL INCLUSIVE"	
[ ] Paternity Establishment (dependent upon cooperation of the Custodial Parent) [ ] Enforcement of court order [ ] Review and Modification	**Full Service Cases Only**
[ ] Collection and Distribution - No Enforcement actions will be taken	

NON-CUSTODIAL APPLICANT IDENTIFYING INFORMATION

Your Name:

Last	First	Middle	Maiden

Social Security Number:

Sex: [ ] Male [ ] Female

Place of Birth:

City	State	County	Country

Eyes: | Hair:

Marital status: [ ] Single [ ] Married
[ ] Separated [ ] Divorced on: _____

Home Address: Do you Own This Property? [ ] Yes [ ] No

Street Address	City	County	State	Zip

Mailing Address:

P O Box	City	County	State	Zip

Do you own a car? Make: _____ Model: _____ Year: _____ TAG# _____

May we contact you at work? [ ] Yes [ ] No

Your relationship to the child(ren): [ ] Biological father [ ] Legal Father [ ] Mother

E-Mail Address:

CUSTODIAL PARENT INFORMATION (Person with whom the child(ren) are living)

Custodial Parent (CP) Name: | Phone Number:

Last	First	Middle	Social Security Number	[ ] Male [ ] Female	Birth Date	Race

CHILD #1 on this case

Last	First	Middle	Social Security Number	[ ] Male [ ] Female	Race

Birth date: | Place of Birth:
| | | CITY | STATE |

CHILD #2 on this case

Last	First	Middle	Social Security Number	[ ] Male [ ] Female	Race

Birth date: | Place of Birth:
| | | CITY | STATE |

CHILD #3 on this case

Last	First	Middle	Social Security Number	[ ] Male [ ] Female	Race

Birth date:	Place of Birth:		
		CITY	STATE

NON-CUSTODIAL APPLICANT INCOME INFORMATION

Employer:				Employed From:	To:	
Address:						
	Street Address	City	County	State	Zip	

Union Member? If so, Local #			Do you have
Salary/Wages/Self employment Income:	$_____		Disability ber
Bonuses, commissions, allowances, overtime, tips, etc	$_____		Worker's Cor
Child Support	$_____		Alimony / Sp
Social Security benefits (SSI, RSDI)	$_____		Unemployme
Pension, retirement, or annuity payments Type: Military, Railroad, VA, etc._____	$_____		Interest, divic 1099 income
Income from royalties, trusts, or estates	$_____		Rental incom

Reimbursed expenses or in-kind payments to the extent that they reduce expenses

Capital gains on sale or exchange of property unless non-recurring income imputed from above assets

Other:_____	$_____	
___		
Bank Name		Account type a
Bank Name		Account type a

NON-CUSTODIAL APPLICANT HEALTH INSURANCE INFORMATION
(if children on this case **are or can be** insured by applicant)

Insurance Co. Name:			Phone No.:		
Address:					
	Street Address	City	County	State	Zip
Policy/Group No.:					
Cost per paycheck for individual coverage: $			For family coverage: $		
Who is presently covered by your insurance?					

NON-CUSTODIAL APPLICANT MONTHLY EXPENSES

Rent or Mortgage	$_____	Utilities (Electric, Gas, Phone)	$_____		
Medical Insurance Premiums	$_____	Child Care	$_____	Other	$_____
Medical Bills or Expenses	$_____	Auto Loan: $_____ Lienholder:_____			

NON-CUSTODIAL APPLICANT FAMILY HISTORY

Mother:			Phone No.:			
Date of Birth:			Deceased on:			
Address:						
	Street Address	City		County	State	Zip
Father:			Phone No.:			
Date of Birth:			Deceased on:			
Address:						
	Street Address	City		County	State	Zip

certify that all of the information supplied by me is true and correct to the best of my knowledge and belief. My gnature on this document constitutes a contract and authorizes the Office of Child Support Enforcement to provide ecessary and appropriate services on my behalf.

understand the criminal penalties for making false statements and false swearing under O.C.G.A. §16-10-71 and do ereby attest to the truthfulness of the information provided.

o sworn and affirmed,

My Signature:_____ Date:_____

Custodian / Custodial Parent Information   This is the person who lives with the child(ren).

CP Name:

| Last | First | Middle | Suffix / Maiden |

Alias, nicknames, etc.:   Sex: [ ] M

Current Marital Status: | If married to someone other than you, current spouse's name:_____
[ ] Single   [ ] Married   [ ] Divorced

Social Security Number: | Date of Birth: (or age, if unknown)

Home Address:

| Street Address | City | County | State | Zip |

Mailing Address:

| P O Box | City | County | State | Zip |

CP Employment and Income Sources

[ ] Unemployed [ ] Self-employed | Type of Business:

Employer: | Phone No.:

Address:

| Street Address | City | County | State | Zip |

CP Health Insurance Information:

Health & Sickness insurance [ ] IS [ ] IS NOT available through CP's employer.

Who is currently covered by Insurance?

Insurance Co. Name: | Phone No.:

Address:

| Street Address | City | County | State | Zip |

Policy/Group No.:

COURT ORDERS, SUPPORT ORDERS, AND ARREARAGE OWED

Note: Check each type of order. You MUST provide a copy of the order(s) to be enforced

[ ] **There is NO Court Order** requiring either parent to pay support for the children of this case, because:

[ ] I am currently married to the CP (no divorce) | Marriage Date:

[ ] I was never married to the CP. (You MUST complete a Paternity Statement for each child of this CP)

[ ] DIVORCE DECREE [ ] OCSE SUPPORT ORDER   [ ] LEGITIMATION ORDER

Filed in   County, State of   on   [ ] No child support ordered.

Support Ordered Amount: $ per   [ ] For each child [ ] For All children

There is an Arrearage (overdue) of $ as of   Complete the attached Arrearage Affidavit*

[ ] CONTEMPT ORDER   [ ] MODIFICATION ORDER

Filed in   County, State of   on   [ ] No child support ordered.

Support Ordered Amount: $ per   [ ] For each child [ ] For All children

There is an Arrearage (overdue) of $ as of   Complete the attached Arrearage Affidavit*

[ ] URESA / UIFSA ORDER (support order from another state)   Note: We must have "certified" copies

Filed in   County, State of   on   [ ] No child support ordered.

Support Ordered Amount: $ per   [ ] For each child [ ] For All children

There is an Arrearage (overdue) of $ as of   Complete the attached Arrearage Affidavit*

Note: If there is more than one court order, an Affidavit of Arrears may need to be completed for each order

Complete this section only if there is a history of domestic violence

Have you ever had any charges filed against you by the CP alleging that you harmed them or your child(ren), either physically or emotionally? [ ] Yes [ ] No

If you said **Yes**, please describe details of any **Restraining Order** or **Protective Orders** below:

Filed in _____ County, State of _____ on _____

Status: [ ] Active; [ ] Dismissed; [ ] Expired on _____

Do you have a child support case with a private attorney or collections agency involving this CP and child(ren)?
If yes, provide contact information:_____

181

CHILD SUPPORT PAYMENT AND ARREARAGE RECORD

Please show the total amount of support **owed and paid to the custodial parent** each month. Receipts, cancel checks, payment records, etc. may be requested to prove the information in this affidavit.

Year	Amount		Year	Amount		Year	Amount	
	Due	Paid		Due	Paid		Due	Paid
Jan	$	$	Jan	$	$	Jan	$	$
Feb	$	$	Feb	$	$	Feb	$	$
Mar	$	$	Mar	$	$	Mar	$	$
Apr	$	$	Apr	$	$	Apr	$	$
May	$	$	May	$	$	May	$	$
Jun	$	$	Jun	$	$	Jun	$	$
Jul	$	$	Jul	$	$	Jul	$	$
Aug	$	$	Aug	$	$	Aug	$	$
Sep	$	$	Sep	$	$	Sep	$	$
Oct	$	$	Oct	$	$	Oct	$	$
Nov	$	$	Nov	$	$	Nov	$	$
Dec	$	$	Dec	$	$	Dec	$	$
YTD Total	$	$	YTD Total	$	$	YTD Total	$	$

Year	Amount		Year	Amount		Year	Amount	
	Due	Paid		Due	Paid		Due	Paid
Jan	$	$	Jan	$	$	Jan	$	$
Feb	$	$	Feb	$	$	Feb	$	$
Mar	$	$	Mar	$	$	Mar	$	$
Apr	$	$	Apr	$	$	Apr	$	$
May	$	$	May	$	$	May	$	$
Jun	$	$	Jun	$	$	Jun	$	$
Jul	$	$	Jul	$	$	Jul	$	$
Aug	$	$	Aug	$	$	Aug	$	$
Sep	$	$	Sep	$	$	Sep	$	$
Oct	$	$	Oct	$	$	Oct	$	$
Nov	$	$	Nov	$	$	Nov	$	$
Dec	$	$	Dec	$	$	Dec	$	$
YTD Total	$	$	YTD Total	$	$	YTD Total	$	$

Total Due:$_____ Minus Total Paid:$_____ = Balance Due: $_____ as of _____

I certify that all of the information supplied by me is true and correct to the best of my knowledge and belief. understand the criminal penalties for making false statements and false swearing under O.C.G.A. §16-10-71 and hereby attest to the truthfulness of the information provided.

So sworn and affirmed,

My Signature:_____ Date: _____

Copies may be made if additional pages are need

PATERNITY STATEMENT

DATE: _____

Case No.:_____

Custodial Parent:_____

_____, being duly sworn by law, willingly and voluntarily
submit to the paternity of the following child(ren) belonging to _____,
(mother) and named as follows:

CHILD(REN)S NAME	CHILD(REN)S D.O.B.
_____	_____
_____	_____
_____	_____

I acknowledge that I have been informed that I have the right to genetic testing, and I have
declined. I submit that this information is complete and correct and I acknowledge that I may be
requested to swear to this fact in a court of law.

NCP Name: _____
(Signature of Parent)
NCP Address: _____

STATE OF GEORGIA, COUNTY OF _____

Personally appeared before me, _____, who being duly
sworn according to law, deposes and says that the above statements are true and were voluntarily
made by him.

Sworn to and Subscribed before me, this ____ day of _____, ___.

Notary Public:_____My Commission Expires:_____

OFFICE OF CHILD SUPPORT ENFORCEMENT

Office Address: _____

City, State Zip: _____

Copies may be made if additional pages are needed

183

INFORMATION I MUST GATHER FOR MY APPLICATION

APPENDIX ONE

GLOSSARY

CHILD SUPPORT ENFORCEMENT TERMS

Accrual – Sum of child support payments that are due or overdue.

Action Transmittal – Document sent out as needed, which instructs state child support programs on the actions they must take to comply with new and amended federal laws. Has basis in federal law and regulation.

Adjudication – The entry of a judgment, decree, or order by a judge or other decision-maker such as a master, referee, or hearing officer based on the evidence submitted by the parties.

Automated Administrative Enforcement of Interstate Cases (AEI) - Provision in the Personal Responsibility and Work Opportunity Reconciliation Act (PRWORA) giving states the ability to locate, place a lien on, and seize financial assets of delinquent obligors across state lines.

Administrative procedure - Method by which support orders are made and enforced by an executive agency rather than by courts and judges.

Administration for Children and Families (ACF) - The agency in the Department of Health and Human Services (DHHS) that houses the Office of Child Support Enforcement (OCSE).

Aid to Families with Dependent Children (AFDC) - Former entitlement program that made public assistance payments on behalf of children who did not have the financial support of one of their parents by reason of death, disability, or continued absence from the home; known in many states as ADC (Aid to Dependent Children). Replaced with Temporary Aid to Needy Families (TANF) under the Personal Responsibility and Work Opportunity Reconciliation Act (PRWORA). (See also: Personal Responsibility and Work Opportunity Reconciliation Act)

Arrearage - Past due, unpaid child support owed by the non-custodial parent. If the parent has arrearages, s/he is said to be "in arrears."

Assignment of support rights - The legal procedure by which a person receiving public assistance agrees to turn over to the state any right to child support, including arrearages, paid by the non-custodial parent in exchange for receipt of a cash assistance grant and other benefits. States can then use a portion of said child support to defray or recoup the public assistance expenditure.

Automated Voice Response System (AVR) - Telephone system that makes frequently requested information available to clients over touch-tone telephones.

B

Burden of Proof - The duty of a party to produce the greater weight of evidence on a point at issue.

C

Case - A collection of people associated with a particular child support order, court hearing, and/or request for IV-D services. This typically includes a custodial parent (CP), a dependent(s), and a noncustodial parent (NCP) and/or putative father (PF). Every child support case has a unique Case ID number and, in addition to names and identifying information about its members, includes information such as CP and NCP wage data, court order details, and NCP payment history. (See also: Child Support; IV-D; IV-D Case; IV-A Case; IV-E Case)

Case initiation - First step in the child support enforcement process.

Case law - Law established by the history of judicial decisions in cases.

Case member - Participant in child support case; a member can participate in more than one case.

Case ID - Unique identification number assigned to a case.

Cash Concentration and Disbursement "Plus" (CCD+) - Standardized format used for electronic funds transmission (EFT) of child support withholdings from an employee's wages. (See also: Electronic Funds Transfer)

Central Registry - A centralized unit, maintained by every State IV-D agency that is responsible for receiving, distributing, and responding to inquiries on interstate IV-D cases.

Centralized Collection Unit - A single, centralized site in each State IV-D agency to which employers can send child support payments they have collected for processing. This centralized payment-processing site is called the State Disbursement Unit (SDU) and is responsible for collecting, distributing, and disbursing child support payments. (See also: State Disbursement Unit)

Child Support - Financial support paid by a parent to help support a child or children of whom they do not have custody. Child support can be entered into voluntarily or ordered by a court or a properly empowered administrative agency, depending on each state's laws. Child support can involve cases where:

, the custodial party (CP) is receiving child support services offered by State and local agencies; (such services include locating a non-custodial parent (NCP) or putative father (PF); establishing paternity; establishing, modifying, and enforcing child support orders; collecting distributing, and disbursing child support payments. (IV-D cases)

, the CP is receiving public assistance benefits and the case is automatically referred to the State Child Support Enforcement CSE) Agency so the State can recoup the cost of the benefits from the non-custodial parent (NCP) or defray future costs. (IV-A cases)

, the child(ren) is being raised not by one of their own parents but in the foster care system by a person, family, or institution and the case is also automatically referred to the CSE to recoup or defray the costs of foster care. (IV-E cases)

(Non IV-D orders)
, the case or legal order is privately entered into and the CSE is not providing locate, enforcement, or collection services (called); often entered into during divorce proceedings. (Non IV-D orders)

The support can come in different forms, including:

   * Medical support, where the child(ren) are provided with health coverage, through private insurance from the non-custodial parent (NCP)
or public assistance that is reimbursed whole or in part by the NCP, or a combination thereof.

   * Monetary payments, in the form of a one-time payment, installments, or regular automatic withholdings from the NCP's income, or the offset of state and/or federal tax refunds and/or administrative payments made to the NCP, such as federal retirement benefits.

There are many tools available to enforce an NCP's obligation. (See also: IV-D; IV-D Case; Non IV-D orders; IV-A; IV-A Case; IV-E; Enforcement)

Child Support Enforcement (CSE) Agency - Agency that exists in every state that locates non-custodial parents (NCPs) or putative fathers (PF), establishes, enforces, and modifies child support, and collects and distributes child support money. Operated by state or local government according to the Child Support Enforcement Program guidelines as set forth in Title IV-D of the Social Security Act. Also known as a "IV-D Agency". (See also: IV-D)

Child Support Enforcement Network (CSENet) - State-to-State telecommunications network, which transfers detailed information between States' automated child support enforcement systems.

Child Support Pass-Through - Provision by which at least $50 from a child support payment collected on behalf of a public assistance recipient is disbursed directly to the custodial parent. The Personal Responsibility and Work Opportunity Reconciliation Act (PRWORA) of 1996 eliminated the pass-through effective October 1, 1996. A few States have elected to retain the pass-through, paying it out of state, rather than federal, money. Also known as Child Support "Disregard." (See also: Public Assistance)

Client - A term often used to refer to the recipient of a TANF grant or IV-D services.

Common Law - A body of law developed from judicial decisions or custom rather than legislative enactments.

Complainant - Person who seeks to initiate court proceedings against another person. In a civil case the complainant is the plaintiff; in a criminal case the complainant is the state.

Complaint - The formal written document filed in a court whereby the complainant sets forth the names of the parties, the allegations, and the request for relief sought. Sometimes called the initial pleading or petition.

CONNECT:Direct (C:D) - Computer network maintained by the Social Security Administration that moves large volumes of data from State agencies and the National Directory of New Hires (NDNH) and the Federal Case Registry (FCR). Formally known as Network Data Mover (NDM).

Consent Agreement - Voluntary written admission of paternity or responsibility for child support.

Consumer Credit Agencies (CCA) - Private agencies that a state can use to locate obligors to establish and enforce child support.

Consumer Credit Protection Act (CCPA) - Federal law that limits the amount that may be withheld from earnings to satisfy child support obligations. States are allowed to set their own limits provided they do not exceed the federal limits. Regardless of the number or withholding orders that have been served, the maximum that may be withheld for child support is:

Without arrearage
50% with a second family
60% Single
With Arrearage
55% with a second family and 12+ weeks in arrears
65% Single 12+ weeks in arrears

Continuing Exclusive Jurisdiction (CEJ) - The doctrine that only one support order should be effective and enforceable between the same parties at any one time and that when a particular court has acquired jurisdiction to determine child support and custody, it retains authority to amend and modify its orders therein. This Court of Continuing Exclusive Jurisdiction (CCEJ) continues to have jurisdiction over a support issue until another court takes it away. Defined in the Uniform Interstate Family Support Act (UIFSA). (See also: Uniform Interstate Family Support Act)

Cooperation - As a condition of TANF eligibility whereby the recipient is required to cooperate with the child support agency in identifying and locating the non-custodial parent, establishing paternity, and/or obtaining child support payments.

Corporate Trade Exchange (CTX) - Standardized format used for electronic funds transmission (EFT) of child support withholdings from employees' wages. This method is preferable when processing large volumes of transactions and PRWORA requires state automated child support enforcement systems to be capable of using this format as well as the CCD+ format.

Court Order - A legally binding edict issued by a court of law. Issued by a magistrate, judge, or properly empowered administrative officer. A court order related to child support can dictate how often, how much, what kind of support a non-custodial parent is to pay, how long he or she is to pay it, and whether an employer must withhold support from their wages.

Custodial Parent (CP) - The person who has primary care, custody, and control of the child(ren).

Custody Order - Legally binding determination that establishes with whom a child shall live. The meaning of different types of custody terms (e.g., joint custody, shared custody, split custody) vary from state to state.

D

Decree - The judicial decision of a litigated action, usually in "equitable" cases such as divorce (as opposed to cases in law in which judgments are entered).

Default - The failure of a defendant to file an answer or appear in a civil case within the prescribed time after having been properly served with a summons and complaint.

Default Judgment - Decision made by the court when the defendant fails to respond

Defendant - The person against whom a civil or criminal proceeding is begun.

Dependent - A child who is under the care of someone else. Most children who are eligible to receive child support must be a dependent. The child ceases to be a dependent when they reach the "age of emancipation" as determined by state law, but depending on the state's provisions, may remain eligible for child support for a period after they are emancipated.

Direct Income Withholding - A procedure, whereby an income withholding order can be sent directly to the non-custodial parent's (NCP's) employer in another state without the need to use the IV-D Agency or court system in the NCP's state. This triggers withholding unless the NCP contests, and no pleadings or registration are required. The Act does not restrict who may send an income withholding notice across state lines. Although the sender will ordinarily be a child support agency or the obligee, the obligor or any other person may supply an employer with an income withholding order. (See also: Income Withholding; Wage Withholding)

Disbursement - The paying out of collected child support funds.

Disclosure Prohibited Notice - A notice that the Federal Case Registry (FCR) is required to send to a party that has requested locate information stating that the information cannot be disclosed because the person being sought has a family violence indicator (FVI) on either a IV-D case or a non IV-D order in the FCR. (See also: Family Violence Indicator)

Disposable Income - The portion of an employee's earnings that remains after deductions required by law (e.g., taxes) and that is used to determine the amount of an employee's pay subject to a garnishment, attachment, or child support withholding order.

Disposition - The court's decision of what should be done about a dispute that has been brought to its attention. For instance, the disposition of the court may be that child support is ordered or an obligation is modified.

Distribution - The allocation of child support collected to the various types of debt within a child support case, as specified in 45 CFR 302.51, (e.g., monthly support obligations, arrears, ordered arrears, etc.).

E

Electronic Data Interchange (EDI) - Process by which information regarding an Electronic Funds Transfer (EFT) transaction is transmitted electronically along with the EFT funds transfer.

Electronic Funds Transfer (EFT) - Process by which money is transmitted electronically from one bank account to another. (See also: Cash Concentration and Disbursement "Plus" (CCD+); Corporate Trade Exchange (CTX)

Enforcement - The application of remedies to obtain payment of a child or medical support obligation contained in a child and/or spousal support order. Examples of remedies include garnishment of wages, seizure of assets, liens placed on assets, revocation of license (e.g., drivers, business, medical, etc.), denial of U.S. passports, etc.

Enumeration and Verification System (EVS) - System used to verify and correct Social Security Numbers (SSNs) and identify multiple SSNs of participants in child support cases. Operated by the Social Security Administration (SSA).

Establishment - The process of proving paternity and/or obtaining a court or administrative order to put a child support obligation in place.

External Locate Source - A source of locate information (that is not part of the Federal Parent Locator Service) on a non-custodial parent (NCP) who works for a Federal Agency.

F

Family Support Act - Law passed in 1988, with two major mandates: Immediate Wage Withholding, unless courts find that there is good cause not require such withholding or there is a written agreement between both parties requiring an alternative arrangement; and Guidelines for Child Support Award Amounts, which requires states to use guidelines to determine the amount of support for each family, unless they are rebutted by a written finding that applying the guidelines would be inappropriate to the case.

Family Violence (FV) Indicator - A designation that resides in the Federal Case Registry (FCR) placed on a participant in a case or order by a state that indicates a person is associated with child abuse or domesticviolence. It is used to prevent disclosure of the location of a custodial party and/or a child believed by the state to be at risk of family violence. (See also: Disclosure Prohibited Notice)

Federal Case Registry (FCR) - A national database of information on individuals in all IV-D cases and all non IV-D orders entered or modified on or after October 1, 1998. The FCR receives this case information on a daily basis from the State Case Registry (SCR) located in every state and proactively matches it with previous submissions to the FCR and with employment information contained in the National Directory of New Hires (NDNH). Any successful matches are returned to the appropriate state(s) for processing. The FCR and the NDNH are both part of the expanded FPLS, which is maintained by OCSE.

Federal Employer Identification Number (FEIN) – Unique nine-digit number assigned to all employers by the Internal Revenue Service (IRS), which must be used in numerous transactions, including submitting data and responding to requests relevant to child support.

Federal Information Processing Standard (FIPS) **Code** - A unique five-digit code that identifies the child support jurisdiction, (i.e., states, counties, central state registries).

Federal Parent Locator Service (FPLS) – A computerized national location network operated by the Federal Office of Child Support (OCSE) of the Administration for Children and Families (ACF), within the Department of Health and Human Services (DHHS). FPLS obtains address and employer information, as well as data on child support cases in every state and compares them and returns matches to the appropriate states. This helps state and local child support enforcement agencies locate non-custodial parents and putative fathers for the purposes of establishing custody and visitation rights, establishing and enforcing child support obligations, investigating parental kidnapping, and processing adoption or foster care cases. The expanded FPLS includes the Federal Case Registry (FCR) and the National Directory of New Hires (NDNH).

Federal Tax Refund Offset Program - Program that collects past due child support amounts from non-custodial parents through the interception of their federal income tax refund, or an administrative payment, such as federal retirement benefits. This program also incorporates the Passport Denial Program, which denies U.S. passports at the time of application when the applicant's child support debts exceed $5,000. In the future, the program will expand to include the revocation and/or restriction of already issued passports. The cooperation of states in the submittal of cases for tax interception is mandatory, while submittal of cases for administrative interception is optional. The Federal Tax Refund Offset Program is operated in cooperation with the Internal Revenue Service, the U.S. Department of Treasury's Financial Management Service (FMS), the U.S. Department of State, and State Child Support Enforcement (CSE) Agencies.

Federally-Assisted Foster Care - A program, funded in part by the Federal government, under which a child is raised in a household by someone other than his or her own parent.

Finding - A formal determination by a court or administrative process that has legal standing.

Foster Care - A federal-state program which provides financial support to a person, family, or institution that is raising a child (or children) who are not their own. (See also: IV-E; IV-E Case)

Full Faith and Credit - Doctrine under which a state must honor an order or judgment entered in another state.

Full Faith and Credit for Child Support Orders Act (FFCCSOA) - Law effective October 20, 1994, which requires states to enforce child support orders made by other states if: the issuing State's tribunal had subject matter jurisdiction to hear and resolve the matter and enter an order; the issuing state's tribunal had personal jurisdiction over the parties; and, reasonable notice and the opportunity to be heard was given to the parties. FFCCSOA also limits a state's ability to modify another states' child support orders in instances when: the state tribunal seeking to modify the order has jurisdiction to do so; and, the tribunal that originally issued the order no longer has continuing, exclusive jurisdiction over the order either because the child and the parties to the case are no longer residents of the issuing State, or the parties to the case have filed written consent to transfer continuing exclusive jurisdiction to be transferred to the tribunal seeking to make the modification. Unlike the Personal Responsibility and Work Opportunity Reconciliation Act of 1996 (PRWORA), FFCCSOA does not amend Title IV-D of the Social Security Act and thus does not directly change IV-D program requirements, but affects interstate case processing. Codified as 28 USC §1738B.

G

Garnishment - A legal proceeding under which part of a person's wages and/or assets is withheld for payment of a debt. This term is usually used to specify that an income or wage withholding is involuntary. (See also: Income Withholding; Wage Withholding; Direct Income Withholding; Immediate Wage Withholding)

Genetic Testing - Analysis of inherited factors to determine legal fatherhood or paternity.

Good Cause - A legal reason for which a Temporary Assistance to Needy Families (TANF) recipient is excused from cooperating with the child support enforcement process, such as past physical harm by the child's father. It also includes situations where rape or incest resulted in the conception of the child and situations where the mother is considering placing the child for adoption. (See also: Temporary Assistance to Needy Families; IV-A Case)

Guidelines - A standard method for setting child support obligations based on the income of the parent(s) and other factors determined by state law. The Family Support Act of 1988 requires states to use guidelines to determine the amount of support for each family, unless they are rebutted by a written finding that applying the guidelines would be inappropriate to the case. (See also: Income; Disposable Income; Imputed Income)

H

HR Bills - Bills introduced in the U.S. House of Representatives begin with the letters "HR."

IV-A ("Four-A") - Reference to Title IV-A of the Social Security Act covering the Federal-State Public Assistance Program.

IV-A Case - A child support case in which a custodial parent and child(ren) is receiving public assistance benefits under the state's IV-A program, which is funded under Title IV-A of the Social Security Act. Applicants for assistance from IV-A programs are automatically referred to their state IV-D agency in order to identify and locate the non-custodial parent, establish paternity and/or a child support order, and/or obtain child support payments. This allows the state to recoup or defray some of its public assistance expenditures with funds from the non-custodial parent. (See also: Temporary Assistance to Needy Families; Public Assistance)

IV-D ("Four-D") - Reference to Title IV-D of the Social Security Act, which required that each state create a program to locate non-custodial parents, establish paternity, establish and enforce child support obligations, and collect and distribute support payments. All recipients of public assistance (usually TANF) are referred to their state's IV-D child support program. States must also accept applications from families who do not receive public assistance, if requested, to assist in collection of child support. Title IV-D also established the Federal Office of Child Support Enforcement.

IV-D Case - A child support case where at least one of the parties, either the custodial party (CP) or the non- custodial parent (NCP), has requested or received IV-D services from the state's IV-D agency. A IV-D case is composed of a custodial party, non-custodial parent, or putative father, and dependent(s).

IV-E ("Four-E") - Reference to Title IV-E of the Social Security Act, which established a federal-state program known as foster care that provides financial support to a person, family, or institution that is raising a child (or children) two who is not their own. The funding for IV-E Foster Care programs is primarily from federal sources. (See also: Foster Care)

IV-E Case - A child support case in which the state is providing benefits or services under Title IV-E of the Social Security Act to a person, family, or institution that is raising a child (or children) who are not their own. As with other public assistance cases, recipients are referred to their state IV-D agency in order to identify and locate the non-custodial parent, establish paternity and/or a child support order, and/or obtain child support payments. This allows the state to recoup or defray some of its public assistance expenditures with funds from the non-custodial parent.

Immediate Wage Withholding - An automatic deduction from income that starts as soon as the agreement for support is established. (See also: Income Withholding; Wage Withholding)

Imputed Income - Fringe benefits provided to employees that may be taxable but which cannot be counted as additional disposable income that is subject to child support obligations. (See also: Disposable Earnings; Guidelines)

Income -As defined by the Personal Responsibility and Work Opportunity Reconciliation Act of 1996 (PRWORA), income is any periodic form of payment to an individual, regardless of source, including wages, salaries, commissions, bonuses, worker's compensation, disability, pension, or retirement program payments and interest. All income (except imputed income; see above) is subject to income withholding for child support, pursuant to a child support order, but is protected by Consumer Credit Protection Act limits, both state and federal. (See also: Consumer Credit Protection Act; Disposable Earnings; Guidelines)

Income Withholding - Procedure by which automatic deductions are made from wages or income, as defined in the Personal Responsibility and Work Opportunity Reconciliation Act (PRWORA), to pay a debt such as child support. Income withholding often is incorporated into the child support order and may be voluntary or involuntary. The provision dictates that an employer must withhold support from a non-custodial parent's wages and transfer that withholding to the appropriate agency (the Centralized Collection Unit or State Disbursement Unit). Sometimes referred to as wage withholding. (See also: Wage Withholding; Direct Income Withholding, a type of interstate Income Withholding; Immediate Wage Withholding)

Information Memorandum (IM) - Document that provides State child support enforcement agencies with information on program practices that can be useful to program improvement.

Initiating Jurisdiction - The state or county court, or administrative agency, which sends a request for action to another jurisdiction in interstate child support cases. The requested action can include a request for wage withholding or for review and adjustment of existing child support obligations. In cases where a state is trying to establish an initial child support order on behalf of a resident custodial parent,

Intercept - A method of securing child support by taking a portion of non-wage payments made to a non-custodial parent. Non-wage payments subject to interception include Federal tax refunds, state tax refunds, unemployment benefits, and disability benefits. (See also: Federal Tax Refund Offset Program)

Interstate Cases - Cases in which the dependent child and non-custodial parent (NCP) live in different States, or where two or more states are involved in some case activity, such as enforcement.

J

Judgment - The official decision or finding of a judge or administrative agency hearing officer upon the respective rights and claims of the parties to an action; also known as a decree or order and may include the "findings of fact and conclusions of law."

Judicial Remedies - A general designation for a court's enforcement of child support obligations.

Jurisdiction - The legal authority which a court or administrative agency has over particular persons and over certain types of cases, usually in a defined geographical area. (See also: Initiating Jurisdiction; Long Arm Jurisdiction)

L

Legal Father - A man who is recognized by law as the male parent of a child.

Lien - A claim upon property to prevent sale or transfer of that property until a debt is satisfied.

Litigation - A civil action in which a controversy is brought before the court.

Locate - Process by which a non-custodial parent (NCP) or putative father (PF) is found for the purpose of establishing paternity, establishing and/or enforcing a child support obligation, establishing custody and visitation rights, processing adoption or foster care cases, and investigating parental kidnapping.

Locate Information - Data used to locate a Putative Father (PF) or non-custodial parent (NCP). May include their Social Security Number (SSN), date of birth (DOB), residential address, and employer.

Long Arm Jurisdiction - Legal provision that permits one State to claim personal jurisdiction over someone who lives in another State. There must be some meaningful connection between the person and the State or district that is asserting jurisdiction in order for a court or agency to reach beyond its normal jurisdictional border. If a Long Arm Statute is not in effect between two States, then the State must undertake a Two-State Action under the Uniform Interstate Family Support Act (UIFSA) guidelines for certain actions, such as establishing a support order in which the non-custodial parent (NCP) is not a resident. Other actions, such as Direct Income Withholding, are allowed by UIFSA in such a way that neither a Two-State Action nor Long Arm Jurisdiction are required. (See also: Two-State Action; Uniform Interstate Family Support Act)

M

Medicaid Program - Federally funded medical support for low income families

Medical Assistance Only (MAO) - Form of public assistance administered by a state's IV-A program, which provides benefits to recipients only in the form of medical, rather than financial, assistance.

Medical Support - Form of child support where medical or dental insurance coverage is paid by the non-custodial parent (NCP). Depending on the court order, medical support can be an NCP's sole financial obligation, or it can be one of several obligations, with child and/or spousal support being the others.

Motion - An application to the court requesting an order or rule in favor of the party that is filing the motion. Motions are generally made in reference to a pending action and may address a matter in the court's discretion or concern a point of law.

Monthly Support Obligation (MSO) - The amount of money an obligor is required to pay per month.

Multi-state Employer - An organization that hires and employs people in two or more states. The multi-state employer conducts business within each state and the employees are required to pay taxes in the state where they work. As with single-state employers, multi-state employers are required by law to report all new hires to the State Directory of New Hires (SDNH) operated by their state government. However, unlike single-state employers, they have the option to report all of their new hires to the SDNH of only one state in which they do business rather than to all of them.

Multi-state Financial Institution Data Match (MSFIDM) - Process created by the Personal Responsibility and Work Opportunity Reconciliation Act (PRWORA) of 1996 by which delinquent child support obligors are matched with accounts held in Financial Institutions (FI) doing business in more than one state. States submit data to the Office of Child Support Enforcement (OCSE) on a non-custodial parent (NCP) and their arrearage and indicate whether the NCP should be submitted for MSFIDM. OCSE ensures the accuracy of the data and transmits the file to participating multi-state financial institutions that match the information against their open accounts and return matches to the appropriate states, which can then undertake action to place a lien on and seize all or part of the account. (See also: Personal Responsibility and Work Opportunity Reconciliation Act (PRWORA) of 1996)

N

National Automated Clearing House Association (NACHA) - The association that establishes the standards, rules, and procedures that enable financial institutions to exchange payments on a national basis.

National Directory of New Hires (NDNH) - A national database containing New Hire (NH) and Quarterly Wage (QW) data from every state and federal agency and Unemployment Insurance (UI) data from State Employment Security Agencies (SESAs). Data contained is first reported to each state's State Directory of New Hires (SDNH) and then transmitted to the NDNH. OCSE maintains the NDNH as part of the expanded FPLS. (See also: New Hire Data; Quarterly Wage Date; Unemployment Insurance Claim Data)

National Personnel Records Center (NPRC) - Part of the National Archives and Records Administration's system of record storage facilities. The NPRC receives and stores both federal Military, and Civilian personnel records.

New Hire (NH) **Data** - Data on a new employee that employers must submit within 20 days of hire to the State Directory of New Hires (SDNH) in the state in which they do business. Minimum information must include the employee's name, address, and Social Security Number (SSN), as well as the employer's name, address, and Federal Employer Identification Number (FEIN). Some states may require or request additional data. Multistate employers have the option of reporting all of their newly hired employees to only one state in which they do business. This data is then submitted to the National Directory of New Hires (NDNH), where it is compared against child support order information contained in the Federal Case Registry (FCR) for possible enforcement of child support obligations by wage garnishment. New hire data may also be used at the state level to find new hires that have been receiving unemployment insurance or other public benefits for which they may no longer be eligible, helping states to reduce waste and fraud. Federal Agencies report this data directly to the NDNH. Also known as (W4) data, after the form used to report the employees. (See also: State Directory of New Hires; National Directory of New Hires)

New Hire Reporting - Program that requires that all employers report newly hired employees to the State Directory of New Hires (SDNH) in their State. This data is then submitted to the National Directory of New Hires (NDNH), where it is compared against child support order information contained in the Federal Case Registry (FCR) for possible enforcement of child support obligations by wage garnishment. Some data is also made available to States to find new hires that have been receiving unemployment insurance or other public benefits for which they may no longer be eligible, helping States to reduce waste and fraud. (See also: State Directory of New Hires; National Directory of New Hires)

Noncustodial Parent (NCP) - The parent who does not have primary care, custody, or control of the child, and has an obligation to pay child support. Also referred to as the obligor. (See also: Custodial Party)

Non IV-A Case - A support case in which the custodial parent has requested IV-D services but is not receiving Temporary Assistance to Needy Families (TANF). Also known as a Non-TANF case.

Non IV-D Orders - A child support order handled by a private attorney as opposed to the State/local child support enforcement (IV-D) agency. (Non-IV-D orders that pre-date January 1, 1994 may be subject to different disbursement requirements.) A non IV-D order is one where the State:

1) Is not currently providing service under the State's Title IV-A, Title IV-D, Title IV-E, or Title XIX programs; has not previously provided state services under any of these programs; and has no current application or applicable fee for services paid by either parent. An IV-D case may become a non IV-D order when: all child support arrearages previously assigned to the state have been paid, and/or the parent(s) originally making application for a state's IV-D services request(s) termination of those IV-D services.

Non IV-D orders established or modified in the State on or after October 1, 1998 must be included in the State Case Registry (SCR) for transmission to the Federal Case Registry (FCR).

A non IV-D order can be converted into IV-D case when the appropriate application and fees for IV-D services are paid by a parent, or when the custodial parent begins receiving Title IV-A services for benefit of the child(ren).

O

Obligated - A term meaning that a non-custodial parent (NCP) is required to meet the financial terms of a court or administrative order.

Obligation - Amount of money to be paid as support by a non-custodial parent (NCP). Can take the form of financial support for the child, medical support, or spousal support. An obligation is a recurring, ongoing obligation, not a onetime debt such as an assessment.

Obligee - The person, state agency, or other institution to which a child support is owed (also referred to as custodial party when the money is owed to the person with primary custody of the child).

Obligor - The person who is obliged to pay child support (also referred to as the non-custodial parent or NCP).

Office of Child Support Enforcement (OCSE) - The federal agency responsible for the administration of the child support program. Created by Title IV-D of the Social Security Act in 1975, OCSE is responsible for the development of child support policy; oversight, evaluation, and audits of State child support enforcement programs; and providing technical assistance and training to the State programs. OCSE operates the Federal Parent Locator Service, which includes the National Directory of New Hires (NDNH) and the Federal Case Registry (FCR). OCSE is part of the Administration for Children and Families (ACF), which is within the Department of Health and Human Services (DHHS).

Office of Personnel Management (OPM) - The federal government's "Human Resources Agency."

Offset - Amount of money intercepted from a parent's state or federal income tax refund, or from an administrative payment such as federal retirement benefits, in order to satisfy a child support debt.

Omnibus Budget Reconciliation Act of 1993 (OBRA '93) - Legislation that mandated that insurance providers and employers offer dependent health coverage to children even if the child is not in the custody of the employee in the plan. OBRA created Qualified Medical Child Support Orders (QMCSOs). (See also: Qualified Medical Child Support Orders)

Order - Direction of a magistrate, judge, or properly empowered administrative officer. (See also: Court Order and Support Order)

Order/Notice to Withhold Child Support - The form to be used by all States that standardizes the information used to request income withholding for child support. According to the Uniform Interstate Family Support Act (UIFSA), this form may be sent directly from the initiating State to a non-custodial parent's employer in another State. (See also: Direct Income Withholding)

P

Passport Denial Program - Program created by the Personal Responsibility and Work Opportunity Reconciliation Act (PRWORA) of 1996 that is operated under the auspices of the Federal Tax Refund Offset Program. Under the Passport Denial Program, obligors with child support arrearages of at least $5000 that are submitted to the to the Federal Office of Child Support Enforcement (OCSE) for Tax Refund Offset are forwarded to the U.S. Department of State, which "flags" the obligor's name and refuses to issue a passport in the event they apply for one. After the obligor makes arrangements to satisfy the arrears, states can decertify them with OCSE, which then requests that the State Department remove them from the program. This program is automatic, meaning that any obligor that is eligible will be submitted to the State Department unless the state submitting the case for tax offset specifically excludes them from the Passport Denial Program. (See also: Federal Tax Refund Offset Program)

Paternity - Legal determination of fatherhood. Paternity must be established before child or medical support can be ordered.

Payee - Person or organization in whose name child support money is paid.

Payor - Person who makes a payment, usually non-custodial parents or someone acting on their behalf, or a custodial party who is repaying a receivable.

Personal Responsibility and Work Opportunity Reconciliation Act of 1996 (PRWORA) - Legislation that provides a number of requirements for employers, public licensing agencies, financial institutions, as well as state and federal child support agencies, to assist in the location of non-custodial parents and the establishment, enforcement, and collection of child support. This legislation created the New Hire Reporting program and the State and Federal Case Registries. Otherwise known as Welfare Reform.

Plaintiff - A person who brings an action; the party who complains or sues in a civil case.

Pleadings - Statements or allegations, presented in logical and legal form, which constitute a plaintiff's cause of action or a defendant's grounds of defense.

Policy Interpretation Question (PIQ) - An official reply by the Federal Office of Child Support Enforcement (OCSE) to an inquiry submitted by a state child support agency concerning application of policy. Although questions often arise from a specific practice or situation, the responses are official statements of OCSE policy on the issue.

Presumption Of Paternity - A rule of law under which evidence of a man's paternity (e.g. voluntary acknowledgment, genetic test results) creates a presumption that the man is the father of a child. A rebuttable presumption can be overcome by evidence that the man is not the father, but it shifts the burden of proof to the father to disprove paternity.

Private Case - Known as a non IV-D case, it is a support case where the custodial parent to whom child support is owed is not receiving IV-A benefits or IV-D services.

Proactive Matching - Process in which child support case data newly submitted to the Federal Case Registry (FCR) is automatically compared with previous submissions, as well as with the employment data in the National Directory of New Hires (NDNH). The resulting locate information is then returned to the appropriate state(s) for processing.

Probability Of Paternity - The probability that the alleged father is the biological father of the child as indicated by genetic test results.

Proceeding - The conduct of business before a judge or administrative hearing officer.

Public Assistance -Benefits granted from State or Federal programs to aid eligible recipients (eligibility requirements vary between particular programs). Applicants for certain types of public assistance (e.g., Temporary Assistance to Needy Families or TANF) are automatically referred to their state IV-D agency identify and locate the non-custodial parent, establish paternity, and/or obtain child support payments. This allows the State to recoup or defray some of its public assistance expenditures with funds from the non-custodial parent.

Putative Father (PF) - The person alleged to be the father of the child but who has not yet been medically or legally declared to be the Legal Father. (See also: Legal Father; Paternity; Genetic Testing)

Q

Qualified Medical Child Support Order (QMCSO) - An order, decree, or judgment, including approval of a settlement agreement, issued by a court or administrative agency of competent jurisdiction that provides for medical support for a child of a participant under a group health plan or provides for health benefit coverage to such child.

Quarterly Wage (QW) **Data** - Data on all employees that must be submitted by employers on a quarterly basis to the State Employment Security Agency (SESA) in the state in which they operate. This data is then submitted to the National Directory of New Hires (NDNH). Minimum information must include the employee's name, address, Social Security Number (SSN), wage amount, and the reporting period as well as the employer's name, address, and Federal Employer Identification Number (FEIN). The data is then compared against child support order information contained in the Federal Case Registry (FCR) for possible enforcement of child support obligations by wage garnishment. Federal Agencies report this data directly to the NDNH. (See also: State Employment Security Agency; National Directory of New Hires)

Quasi-Judicial - A framework or procedure under the auspices of a state's judicial branch in which court officers other than judges process, establish, enforce and modify support orders, usually subject to judicial review. The court officer may be a magistrate, a clerk, master, or court examiner. He or she may or may not have to be an attorney, depending on the state's law.

R

Recipient - A person or organization that receives support funds and/or Temporary Assistance to Needy Families (TANF) payments. (See also: Temporary Assistance to Needy Families (TANF); IV-A; IV-A Case; Public Assistance)

Reciprocity - A relationship in which one state grants certain privileges to other states on the condition that they receive the same privilege.

Referral - Request sent to a IV-D agency from a non IV-D agent or agency asking that a child support case be established.

Respondent - The party answering a petition or motion.

Responding Jurisdiction - The court or administrative agency with jurisdiction over a non-custodial parent or child support order on which an initiating state has requested action.

Review and Adjustment - Process in which current financial information is obtained from both parties in a child support case and evaluated to decide if a support order needs to be adjusted.

Revised Uniform Reciprocal Enforcement of Support Act (RURESA) - Revised URESA law that sets forth reciprocal laws concerning the enforcement of child support between States. (See also: Uniform Reciprocal Enforcement of Support Act; Uniform Interstate Family Support Act)

S

Service of Process - The delivery of a writ or summons to a party for the purpose of obtaining jurisdiction over that party.

Service by Publication - Service of process accomplished by publishing a notice in a newspaper or by posting on a bulletin board of a courthouse or other public facility, after a court determines that other means of service are impractical or have been unsuccessful. This procedure is not legal in every state.

Show Cause - A court order directing a person to appear and bring forth any evidence as to why the remedies stated in the order should not be confirmed or executed. A show cause order is usually based on a motion and affidavit asking for relief.

Single State Financial Institution Data Match - Process by which delinquent child support obligors are matched with accounts held in financial institutions (FI) doing business in only one state.

Spousal Support - Court ordered support of a spouse or ex-spouse; also referred to as maintenance or alimony.

State Case Registry (SCR) - A database maintained by each state that contains information on individuals in all IV-D cases and all non IV-D orders established or modified after October 1, 1998. Among the data included in the SCR are the state's numerical FIPS code; the state's identification number (which must be unique to the case); the case type (IV-D vs. Non IV-D); and locate information on persons listed in the case, in addition to other information. Information submitted to the SCR is transmitted to the Federal Case Registry, where it is compared to cases submitted to the FCR by other states, as well as the employment data in the National Directory of New Hires (NDNH). Any matches found are returned to the appropriate states for processing. (See also: Federal Case Registry; IV-D Case; Non IV-D Order)

State Directory of New Hires - A database maintained by each state, which contains information regarding newly hired employees for the respective state. The data is then transmitted to the NDNH, where it is compared to the employment data from other states, as well as child support data in the Federal Case Registry (FCR). Any matches found are returned to the appropriate states for processing. Employers are required to submit new hire data to the SDNH within 20 days of the hire date. Multi-state employers (those that do business and hire workers in more than one state) have additional options on where to report new hire information. In most states, the SDNH is contained in the State Parent Locator Service (SPLS) that is part of each state IV-D agency, in others it is operated by the State Employment Security Agency (SESA). (See also: National Directory of New Hires; New Hire Reporting Program)

State Disbursement Unit (SDU) - The single site in each state where all child support payments are processed. Upon implementation of centralized collections, each state will designate its State Disbursement Unit, or SDU, to which all withheld child support payments should be sent.

State Employment Security Agency (SESA) - Agencies in each state that process unemployment insurance claims. They are also repositories of quarterly wage data, information on all employees submitted by employers, which they submit to the National Directory of New Hires (NDNH) along with the unemployment insurance claim data. In some states, the SESA also operates the State Directory of New Hires (SDNH), which contains data submitted by employers on newly hired employees. Data submitted to the NDNH is then compared against child support order information contained in the Federal Case Registry (FCR) for possible enforcement of child support obligations by wage garnishment. (See also: Unemployment Insurance Claim Data; Quarterly Wage Data; New Hire Data; State Directory of New Hires;

National Directory of New Hires)

State Parent Locator Services (SPLS) - A unit within the state Child Support Enforcement Agencies the purpose of which is to locate noncustodial parents in order to establish and enforce child support obligations, visitation, and custody orders or to establish paternity. This unit operates the State Case Registry (SCR), and in most States, the State Directory of New Hires (SDNH). (In some States the SDNH is operated by the State Employment Security Agency or SESA.)

Standardized Data Elements - Data elements that must be included in each child support case record that is transmitted to the Federal Case Registry (FCR).

Statute Of Limitations - The period during which someone can be held liable for an action or a debt. Statutes of limitations for collecting child support vary from state to state

Stay - An order by a court that suspends all or some of the proceedings in a case.

Support Order - A judgment, decree, or order, whether temporary, final, or subject to modification, issued by a court or an administrative agency of a competent jurisdiction, for the support and maintenance of a child. This includes a child who has attained the age of majority under the law of the issuing state, or of the parent with whom the child is living. Support orders can incorporate the provision of monetary support, health care, payment of arrearages, or reimbursement of costs and fees, interest and penalties, and other forms of relief. (See also: Obligation; Non-custodial Parent; Obligor)

Subpoena - A process issued by a court compelling a witness to appear at a judicial proceeding. Sometimes the process will also direct the witness to bring documentary evidence to the court.

Summons - A notice to a defendant that an action against him or her has been commenced in the court issuing the summons and that a judgment will be taken against him or her if the complaint is not answered within a certain time.

T

Temporary Assistance to Needy Families (TANF) - Time-limited public assistance payments made to poor families, based on Title IV-A of the Social Security Act. TANF replaced Aid to Families with Dependent

Children (AFDC— otherwise known as welfare) when the Personal Responsibility and Work Opportunity Reconciliation Act (PRWORA) was signed into law in 1996. The program provides parents with job preparation, work, and support services to help them become self-sufficient. Applicants for TANF benefits are automatically referred to their state IV-D agency in order to establish paternity and child support for their children from the non-custodial parent. This allows the state to recoup or defray some of its public assistance expenditures with funds from the non-custodial parent. (See also: Personal Responsibility and Work Opportunity Reconciliation Act)

Third Party Liability - A category under which the state pays the difference between the amount of the medical bill and the amount the insurance company has paid. This occurs only when a public assistance recipient has medical insurance in addition to coverage provided by the public assistance program.

Tribunal - The court, administrative agency, or quasi-judicial agency authorized to establish or modify support orders or to determine parentage.

Two-State Action - Action a state must file under the Uniform Interstate Family Support Act (UIFSA) guidelines when it does not have Long Arm Jurisdiction (i.e., cannot legally claim personal jurisdiction over a non-custodial parent who lives in another state). This is usually in cases where a state is trying to establish an initial child support order on behalf of a resident custodial party. Other actions, such as requesting wage withholding or reviewing and/or revising an existing support order, do not require a Two-State Action even if the initiating state does not have Long Arm Jurisdiction. (See also: Initiating Jurisdiction; Two-State Action; Uniform Interstate Family Support Act)

U

Unclaimed Funds - Support payment that cannot be disbursed because the identity of the payor is unknown or the address of the payee is unknown.

Unemployment Insurance (UI) **Claim Data** - Data on unemployment insurance and applicants claimants submitted by State Employment Security Agencies (SESAs) on a quarterly basis to the National Directory of New Hires (NDNH). Minimum information must include the employee's name, address, Social Security Number (SSN), the benefit amount, and reporting period. This data is then compared against child support order information contained in the Federal Case Registry (FCR) for possible enforcement of child support obligations by garnishment. (See also: State Employment Security Agency; National Directory of New Hires) Uniform Interstate Family Support Act (UIFSA) - Laws enacted at the state level to provide mechanisms for establishing and enforcing child support obligations in interstate cases (when a non-custodial parent lives in a different state than his/her child and the custodial party). Based on model legislation that was drafted by the National Conference of Commissioners on Uniform State Laws to revise and replace URESA. The provisions of UIFSA supercede those of URESA, although some URESA provisions may remain in effect (some states have rescinded all of URESA, while others have left in place those provisions not specifically superceded by UIFSA). Among the law's provisions is the ability of State IV-D agencies to send withholding orders to employers across state lines (see also Direct Income Withholding). PRWORA mandated that all states adopt legislation requiring that UIFSA be adopted, without modification by the state, January 1, 1998.

Uniform Reciprocal Enforcement of Support Act (URESA) - Law first promulgated in 1950 which provides a mechanism for establishing, enforcing, and modifying support obligations in interstate cases. Has now been superceded by the Uniform Interstate Family Support Act (UIFSA).

Unreimbursed Public Assistance (UPA) - Money paid in the form of public assistance (for example, TANF or older AFDC expenditures) which has not yet been recovered from the non-custodial parent (NCP).

V

Visitation - The right of a non-custodial parent to visit or spend time with his or her children.

Voluntary Acknowledgement Of Paternity - An acknowledgement by a man, or both parents, that the man is the father of a child, usually provided in writing on an affidavit or form.

W

Wage Assignment - A voluntary agreement by an employee to transfer (or assign) portions of future wage payments (e.g., insurance premium deductions, credit union deductions) to pay certain debts, such as child support.

Wage Attachment - An involuntary transfer of a portion of an employee's wage payment to satisfy a debt. In some states, this term is used interchangeably with Wage or Income Withholding. In other states, there are distinctions between an attachment and withholding. The most common term used is Wage or Income Withholding. (See also: Wage Withholding and Income Withholding)

Wage Withholding - A procedure by which scheduled deductions are automatically made from wages or income to pay a debt, such as child support. Wage withholding often is incorporated into the child support order and may be voluntary or involuntary. The provision dictates that an employer must withhold support from a non-custodial parent's wages and transfer that withholding to the appropriate agency (the Centralized Collection Unit or State Disbursement Unit). Also known as income withholding. (See also: Income Withholding; Direct Income Withholding)

ACRONYMS

ACF - Administration for Children and Families
AEI - Automated Administrative Enforcement of Interstate Cases
AFDC - Aid to Families with Dependent Children
AT - Action Transmittal
AVR - Automated Voice Response System
CCA - Consumer Credit Agencies
CCD+ - Cash Concentration and Disbursement "Plus"
CCPA - Consumer Credit Protection Act
CEJ - Continuing Exclusive Jurisdiction to modify a support order
C:D - CONNECT:Direct
CP - Custodial Parent
CSE - Child Support Enforcement Agency
CSENet - Child Support Enforcement Network
CTX - Corporate Trade Exchange
DCL - Dear Colleague Letter
DHHS - United States Department of Health and Human Services
DOB - Date of Birth
EDI - Electronic Data Interchange
EFT - Electronic Funds Transfer
EVS - Enumeration and Verification System
FCR - Federal Case Registry of Child Support Orders
FEIN - Federal Employer Identification Number
FFCCSOA - Full Faith and Credit for Child Support Orders Act
FIPS - Federal Information Processing Standards
FMS - Financial Management Service
FPLS - Federal Parent Locator Service
FSA - Family Support Act
FVI - Family Violence Indicator
IM - Information Memorandum
IRS - Internal Revenue Service
IV-A - Title IV-A of the Social Security Act
IV-D - Title IV-D of the Social Security Act
IV-E - Title IV-E of the Social Security Act
MAO - Medical Assistance Only
MSFIDM - Multi-state Financial Institution Data Match
MSO - Monthly Support Obligation
NACHA - National Automated Clearing House Association
NCP - Non-Custodial Parent
NDM - Network Data Mover
NDNH - National Directory of New Hires
NH - New Hire
NPRC - National Personnel Records Center
OCSE - Federal Office of Child Support Enforcement
OPM - Office of Personnel Management
PF - Putative Father

PIQ - Policy Interpretation Question
PRWORA - Personal Responsibility and Work Opportunity Reconciliation Act of 1996
QW - Quarterly Wage
RURESA - Revised Uniform Reciprocal Enforcement of Support Act
SCR - State Case Registry of Child Support Orders
SDNH - State Directory of New Hires
SDU - State Disbursement Unit
SESA - State Employment Security Agency
SPLS - State Parent Locator Service
SSA - Social Security Administration
SSN - Social Security Number
SPLS - State Parent Locator Service
TANF - Temporary Assistance for Needy Families
UI - Unemployment Insurance
UIFSA - Uniform Interstate Family Support Act
UPA - Unreimbursed Public Assistance
URESA - Uniform Reciprocal Enforcement of Support Act

NOTES

APPENDIX TWO

ADDRESSES FOR WORLDWIDE LOCATOR SERVICES (FOR MILITARY ADDRESS)

Army Active Duty
Army Worldwide Locator
USAEREC
8899 E. 56th Street
Indianapolis, IN 46249
(703) 325-3732 Navy

Navy Personnel Command
(Pers 312)
5720 Integrity Drive
Millington, TN 38055-3120
(901) 874-3388

Coast Guard
Commander (MPC-53)
U.S. Coast Guard
2100 2nd St. SW
Washington DC 20593
(202) 267-1340 Army Reserve/Retired

Commander
ARPERCEN
9700 Page Blvd.
St Louis, MO 63132
(314) 538-3777

Air Force
Headquarters
AFMPC/RMIQL
550 C St. West, Suite 50
Randolph AFB, TX 78150
(210) 652-5774/5775/6377 Marine Corps

Headquarters, U.S.M.C.
Code MMSB-10
2008 Elliot Rd., Rm. 201
Quantico, VA 22134
(703) 784-3942

Note: Civilian requesters, including state and local officials and agents, must submit requests in writing, preferably on office letterhead. Appendix C is a sample letter requesting a member's home address.

NOTES

SAMPLE LETTER TO REQUEST LOCATOR SERVICES

[Your agency or office letterhead]

[WMLS Address from Appendix A]

Re: SGT John Jones, SSN: 123-45-6789

Dear Sir or Madam:

Please advise me of the military unit and duty station address for the referenced individual, whom I believe to be an active duty member of the [Army, Navy, etc]. The information should be sent to my attention at the letterhead address. Alternatively, a telephonic response is acceptable. My office phone number is (000) 123-4567.

This request is made in my official capacity as a child support enforcement agent for [county, state, etc]. Since we are a public agency, I request that the normal fee for this information be waived. If you need any further information regarding this request, please call me.

Sincerely,

Dawnette Lounds-Culp

SAMPLE LETTER TO REQUEST HOME ADDRESS

[Your office or agency letterhead]

Commander, Fort Blank
Attn: Military Personnel Officer
Fort Blank, CA 98765-4321

Re: SGT John Jones, SSN: 123-45-6789

Dear Sir or Madam:

This request is submitted pursuant to the Freedom of Information Act. I request to be advised of the named member's home address. Since I am the head of a [state] [county] governmental agency engaged in a civil and/or criminal law enforcement activity in this matter, as authorized by state law, I believe that the requested disclosure constitutes a routine use of this information from the member's personnel records.

Additionally, I believe this information is generally releasable in this case under FOIA, notwithstanding the Privacy Act. I am acting in my capacity as the head of a public law enforcement agency on a matter involving the establishment and enforcement of this member's child support obligation, and I require a home address to fully discharge my responsibilities under state law. The public interest in disclosure to achieve child support enforcement outweighs the member's privacy interests, and therefore release would not constitute an unreasonable invasion of privacy.

The information is sought by a public agency; it will not be used for commercial purposes or for anyone's commercial gain. In view of this fact, and since the search should not require more than 2 hours and fewer than 100 pages are being requested, I assume there will be no chargeable search and reproduction fees. If fees must be assessed, however, please notify me so I can make appropriate arrangements.

I certify that I am authorized by law to collect this information. Please send your response to my attention at the letterhead address. If you need any further information in order to process this request, please call me at (area code) number.

Sincerely,

(This letter should be signed by the director of a law enforcement agency)

For Army Retirees send letter to: U.S. Army Community and Family Support Center, Retired &Veterans Affairs Division, ATTN: DACF-IS-RV, Alexandria, VA 22331-0522

ADDITIONAL SOURCES OF ASSISTANCE IN ENFORCING SUPPORT

Army
Office of the Judge Advocate General
ATTN: DAJA-LA
2200 Army Pentagon
Washington DC 20310
(703) 697-3170 Navy

Bureau of Naval Personnel
Office of Legal Counsel
(Pers O6)
2 Navy Annex
Washington DC 20370-5006
(703) 325-7928

Marine Corps
Paralegal Specialist
Headquarters, U.S. Marine Corps (JAR)
2 Navy Annex
Washington DC 20380
(703) 614-3880 Air Force

AFLSA/JACA
1420 Air Force Pentagon
Washington DC 20330-1420
(703) 697-0413

Coast Guard
United States Coast Guard
G-PC (USCG)
Room 4100E, CGHQ
Department of Transportation
Washington, DC 20590
(202) 267-2799

The agency points of contact listed above are designated officials responsible for facilitating the service of legal process on members of the Uniformed Services. They may also provide useful assistance in resolving problems created by a nonresponsive chain of command.

Tips for using these agencies:

1. Write the member's commander first.

2. Provide the member's name and Social Security Number.

3. Give specific facts on periods of nonsupport or other problems. Note your previous efforts to resolve the issues and state how the results were unsatisfactory.

4. State clearly the relief you seek. These agencies will ensure the command is aware of the problem and that the member is counseled regarding support obligations.

NOTES

APPENDIX THREE

WEBSITES, ADDRESSES AND TELEPHONE NUMBERS

Angel Eyes Publishing Co.
3206 Shadow Walk Lane
Suite A
Tucker, GA 30084
www.angeleyespublishingco.com
(404) 423-5476

PRO-YOUTH INC.
3206 Shadow Walk Lane
Suite B
Tucker, GA 30084
www.pro-youthinc.org
(404) 423-5476

Federal Office of Child Support Enforcement
www.acf.hhs.gov/programs/cse

CHILD SUPPORT ENFORCEMENT OFFICES ADDRESSES AND TELEPHONE NUMBERS

*In-State Only
**Nationwide

ALABAMA
Department of Human Resources
Division of Child Support
50 Ripley Street
Montgomery, AL 36130-1801
(334) 242-9300
FAX: (334) 242-0606
1-800-284-4347 *

ALASKA
Child Support Enforcement Division
550 West 7th Avenue, Suite 310
Anchorage, AK 99501-6699
(907) 269-6900
FAX: (907) 269-6813
1-800-478-3300 *

ARIZONA
Division of Child Support Enforcement
P. O. Box 40458
Phoenix, AZ 85067
(602) 252-4045
(no toll-free number)

ARKANSAS
Office of Child Support Enforcement
P.O. Box 8133
Little Rock, AR 72203
Street Address: 712 West Third
Little Rock, AR 72201
(501) 682-8398
FAX: (501) 682-6002
1-800-264-2445** (Payments)
1-800-247-4549** (Program)

CALIFORNIA
Office of Child Support
Department of Social Services
P. O. Box 944245
Sacramento, CA 95244-2450
(916) 654-1532
FAX: (916) 657-3791
1-800-952-5253*

COLORADO
Division of Child Support Enforcement
1575 Sherman Street, 2nd Floor
Denver, CO 80203-1714
(303) 866-5994
FAX: (303) 866-3574
(no toll-free number)

CONNECTICUT
Department of Social Services
Bureau of Child Support Enforcement
25 Sigourney Street
Hartford, CT 06106-5033
(860) 424-5251
FAX: (860) 951-2996
1-800-228-5437** (problems)
1-800-647-8872** (information)
1-800-698-0572** (payments)

DELAWARE
Division of Child Support Enforcement
Delaware Health and Social Services
1901 North Dupont Hwy
P.O. Box 904
New Castle, DE 19720
(302) 577-4863, 577-4800
FAX: (302) 577-4873
(no toll-free number)

DISTRICT OF COLUMBIA
Office of Paternity and
Child Support Enforcement
Department of Human Services
800 9th Street, SW, 2nd Floor
Washington, DC 20024-2485
(202) 645-7500
(no toll-free number)

FLORIDA
Child Support Enforcement Program
Department of Revenue
P.O. Box 8030
Tallahassee, FL 32314-8030
(850) 922-9590
FAX: (850) 488-4401
(no toll-free number)

GEORGIA
Child Support Administration
P.O. Box 38450
Atlanta, GA 30334-0450
(404) 657-3851
FAX: (404) 657-3326
1-800-227-7993* (for 706 & 912 area codes)
from area codes 404 & 770, dial code + 657-2780)

GUAM
Department of Law
Child Support Enforcement Office
238 Archbishop F.C. Flores, 7th Floor
Agana, GU 96910
(671) 475-3360
(no toll-free number)

HAWAII
Child Support Enforcement Agency
Department of Attorney General
680 Iwilei Street, Suite 490
Honolulu, HI 96817
(808) 587-3698
(no toll-free number)

IDAHO
Bureau of Child Support Services
Department of Health and Welfare
450 West State Street, 5th Floor
Boise, ID 83720 - 5005
(208) 334-5710
FAX: (208) 334-0666
1-800-356-9868**

ILLINOIS
Child Support Enforcement Division
Illinois Department of Public Aid
509 South Sixth
Mariott Building
P. O. Box 19405
Springfield, IL 62701-1825
(217) 524-4602
FAX: (217) 524-4608
1-800-447-4278*

INDIANA
Child Support Office
402 West Washington Street, Rm W360
Indianapolis, IN 46204
(317) 233-5437
FAX: (317) 233-4925
1-800-622-4932**

IOWA
Bureau of Collections
Department of Human Services
Hoover Building - 5th Floor
Des Moines, IA 50319
(515) 281-5580
FAX: (515) 281-8854
(no toll-free number)

KANSAS
Child Support Enforcement Program
Department of Social & Rehabilitation Services
P.O. Box 497
Topeka, KS 66601
Street Address: 300 S.W. Oakley Street,
Biddle Building
Topeka, KS 66606
(913) 296-3237
FAX: (913) 296-5206
1-800-432-0152 (Withholding)
1-800-570-6743 (Collections)
1-800-432-3913 (Fraud Hotline)

KENTUCKY
Division of Child Support Enforcement
Cabinet for Families and Children
P. O. Box 2150
Frankfort, KY 40602
(502) 564-2285
FAX: (502) 564-5988

LOUISIANA
Support Enforcement Services
Office of Family Support
P.O. Box 94065
Baton Rouge, LA 70804-4065
(504) 342-4780
FAX: (504) 342-7397
1-800-256-4650* (Payments)   237

MAINE
Division of Support Enforcement and Recovery
Bureau of Family Independence
Department of Human Services
State House Station 11 Whitten Road
Augusta, ME 04333
(207) 287-2886
FAX: (207) 287-5096
1-800-371-3101*

MARYLAND
Child Support Enforcement Administration
Department of Human Resources
311 West Saratoga Street
Baltimore, MD 21201
(410) 767-7619
FAX: (410) 333-8992
1-800-332-6347*

MASSACHUSETTS
Child Support Enforcement Division
Department of Revenue
141 Portland Street
Cambridge, MA 02139-1937
FAX: (617) 621-4991
1-800-332-2733**

MICHIGAN
Office of Child Support
Department of Social Services
P.O. Box 30478
Lansing, MI 48909-7978
Street Address: 7109 W. Saginaw Hwy.
Lansing, MI 48909-7978
(517) 373-7570
FAX: (517) 373-4980
(no toll-free number)

MINNESOTA
Office of Child Support Enforcement
Department of Human Services
444 Lafayette Road, 4th floor
St. Paul, MN 55155-3846
(612) 215-1714
FAX: (612) 297-4450
(no toll-free number)

MISSISSIPPI
Division of Child Support Enforcement
Department of Human Services
P.O. Box 352
Jackson, MS 39205
(601) 359-4861
FAX: (601) 359-4415
1-800-434-5437(Jackson)**
1-800-354-6039 (Hines, Rankin
(and Madison Counties)

MISSOURI
Department of Social Services
Division of Child Support Enforcement
P.O. Box 2320
Jefferson City, MO 65102-2320
(573) 751-4301
FAX: (573) 751-8450

MONTANA
Child Support Enforcement Division
Department of Public Health and Human Services
P.O. Box 202943
Helena, MT 59620
(406) 442-7278
1-800-346-5437*

NEBRASKA
Child Support Enforcement Office
Department of Social Services
P.O. Box 95044
Lincoln, NE 68509
(402) 471-9160
FAX: (402) 471-9455
1-800-831-4573*

NEVADA
Child Support Enforcement Program
Nevada State Welfare Division
2527 North Carson Street
Carson City, NV 89706-0113
(702) 687-4744
FAX: (702) 684-8026
1-800-992-0900*

NEW HAMPSHIRE
Office of Child Support
Division of Human Services
Health and Human Services Building
6 Hazen Drive
Concord, NH 03301-6531
(603) 271-4427
FAX: (603) 271-4787
1-800-852-3345* ext. 4427

NEW JERSEY
Division of Family Development
Department of Human Services
Bureau of Child Support and
Paternity Programs
P.O. Box 716
Trenton, NJ 08625-0716
(609) 588-2915
FAX: (609) 588-3369
1-800-621-5437**

NEW MEXICO
Child Support Enforcement Bureau
Department of Human Services
P.O. Box 25109
Santa Fe, NM 87504
Street Address: 2025 S. Pacheco
Santa Fe, NM 87504
(505) 827-7200
FAX: (505) 827-7285

NEW YORK
Office of Child Support Enforcement
Department of Social Services
P.O. Box 14
One Commerce Plaza
Albany, NY 12260-0014
(518) 474-9081
FAX: (518) 486-3127
1-800-343-8859*

NORTH CAROLINA
Child Support Enforcement Office
Division of Social Services
Department of Human Resources
100 East Six Forks Road
Raleigh, NC 27609-7750
(919) 571-4114
FAX: (919) 881-2280
1-800-992-9457*

NORTH DAKOTA
Department of Human Services
Child Support Enforcement Agency
P.O. Box 7190
Bismarck, ND 58507-7190
(701) 328-3582
FAX: (701) 328-5497
1-800-755-8530*

OHIO
Office of Family Assistance and
Child Support Enforcement
Department of Human Services
30 East Broad Street - 31st Floor
Columbus, OH 43266-0423
(614) 752-6561
FAX: (614) 752-9760
1-800-686-1556

OKLAHOMA
Child Support Enforcement Division
Department of Human Services
P.O. Box 53552
Oklahoma City, OK 73152
Street Address: 2409 N. Kelley Avenue
Annex Building
Oklahoma City, OK 73111
(405) 522-5871
FAX: (405) 522-2753
1-800-522-2922**

OREGON
Recovery Services Section
Adult and Family Services Division
Department of Human Resources
260 Liberty Street N.E.
Salem, OR 97310
(503) 378-5567
FAX: (503) 391-5526
1-800-850-0228*

PENNSYLVANIA
Bureau of Child Support Enforcement
Department of Public Welfare
P.O. Box 8018
Harrisburg, PA 17105
(717) 787-3672
FAX: (717) 787-9706
1-800-932-0211**

PUERTO RICO
Child Support Enforcement
Department of Social Services
P.O. Box 9023349
San Juan, PR 00902-3349
Street Address: Majagua Street, Bldg. 2
Wing 4, 2nd Floor
Rio Pedras, PR 00902-9938
(787) 767-1500
FAX: (787) 282-7411
(no toll-free number)

RHODE ISLAND
Child Support Services
Division of Administration and
Taxation
77 Dorrance Street
Providence, RI 02903
(401) 277-2847
FAX: (401) 277-6674
1-800-638-5437*

SOUTH CAROLINA
Department of Social Services
Child Support Enforcement Division
P.O. Box 1469
Columbia, SC 29202-1469
(803) 737-5875
FAX: (803) 737-6032
1-800-768-5858**
1-800-768-6779*(Payments)

SOUTH DAKOTA
Office of Child Support Enforcement
Department of Social Services
700 Governor's Drive
Pierre, SD 57501-2291
(605) 773-3641
FAX: (605) 773-5246
(no toll-free number)

TENNESSEE
Child Support Services
Department of Human Services
Citizens Plaza Building - 12th Floor
400 Deadrick Street
Nashville, TN 37248-7400
(615) 313-4880
FAX: (615) 532-2791
1-800-838-6911* (Payments)

TEXAS
Office of the Attorney General
State Office
Child Support Division
P.O. Box 12017
Austin, TX 78711-2017
(512) 460-6000
FAX: (512) 479-6478
1-800-252-8014**

UTAH
Office of Recovery Services
P.O. Box 45011
Salt Lake City, UT 84145-0011
(801) 536-8500
FAX: (801) 436-8509
1-800-257-9156**

VERMONT
Office of Child Support
103 South Main Street
Waterbury, VT 05671-1901
FAX: (802) 244-1483
1-800-786-3214**

VIRGIN ISLANDS
Paternity and Child Support Division
Department of Justice
GERS Building, 2nd Floor
48B-50C Krondprans Gade
St. Thomas, VI 00802
(809) 775-3070
FAX: (809) 775-3808
(no toll-free number)

VIRGINIA
Division of Child Support Enforcement
Department of Social Services
730 East Broad Street
Richmond, VA 23219
(804) 692-1428
FAX: (804) 692-1405
1-800-468-8894*

WASHINGTON
Division of Child Support
Department of Social Health Services
P.O. Box 9162
Olympia, WA 98504-9162
Street Address: 712 Pear St., S.E
Olympia, WA 98504
(360) 586-3162
FAX: (206) 586-3274
1-800-457-6202**

WEST VIRGINIA
Child Support Enforcement Division
Department of Health & Human Resources
1900 Kanawha Boulevard East
Capitol Complex, Building 6, Room 817
Charleston, WV 25305
(304) 558-3780
1-800-249-3778**

WISCONSIN
Bureau of Child Support
Division of Economic Support
P.O. Box 7935
Madison, WI 53707-7935
Street Address: 201 E. Washington Ave. Room 271
Madison, WI 53707
(608) 266-9909
FAX: (608) 267-2824
(no toll-free number)

WYOMING
Child Support Enforcement
Department of Family Services
2300 Capital Avenue, 3rd Floor
Cheyenne, WY 82002-0490
(307) 777-6948
FAX: (307) 777-3693
(no toll-free number)

ABOUT THE AUTHOR

Dawnette Lounds-Culp is a custodial parent who has mastered the child support process by extensively researching the child support process by extensively researching the child support enforcement process. Fed up with the broken promises of the father of her now ten-year-old, she sought support for her son. <u>The Face of Child Support</u> is a compilation of what she learned while navigating the system.

Currently married and the mother of another son, Dawnette says, "I have a wonderful husband, who, too, grew up on the child support system. Steven's memories were similar to mine and in writing this book, he has encouraged me and been my support.

The title, "The Face of Child Support," represents not only the children involved in the child support process, but also the custodial and noncustodial parents and other adults who are products of the child support system.

Dawnette Lounds-Culp is the founder of PRO-YOUTH, INC., a nonprofit organizations that is a positive reinforcement on youth. The organization provides meetings, workshops, programs, and events for youth to become involved in. For further information checkout the website at www.pro-youthinc.us.